TAXES FOR SMALL BUSINESSES 2021

THE BLUEPRINT TO UNDERSTANDING TAXES FOR YOUR LLC, SOLE PROPRIETORSHIP, STARTUP AND ESSENTIAL STRATEGIES AND TIPS TO REDUCE YOUR TAXES LEGALLY

BRANDON'S BUSINESS GUIDES

CONTENTS

INTRODUCTION

Hello, there! Thank you for taking the time to join us! We are going to go on a fabulous journey in the world of small business and the taxes and processes that come along with being a small business owner.

As a small business owner, you know first hand that when it comes to taxes, there is no such thing as simple. The tax code can be a challenge to navigate for even the most business savvy of us all. It's not uncommon for people to miss out on things such as deductions or credits that could have saved them thousands. Or even worse, end up with errors or late returns that cost you extra in fees and fines, and let's face it, any unexpected cost in a small business can throw things out of whack in a snap.

In this guidebook, we will help you understand all of the basics you need to know about taxes as a small business owner, and give you strategies to lower your taxes in a legal way.

We'll go over Tax Basics first so to start off with, you'll have the groundwork in your mind for the more detailed info, as well as some of the common terminology associated with Taxation and Accounting. Then, we can't talk taxes without the good ol' IRS, so we've dedicated a chapter to the agency to give you a little bit of history and background on what exactly it is that they do there.

The next few chapters will be filled with important information that is specific to your small business taxes, including some great tips and tricks to help you out along the way. Then finally, we'll end with discussing Tax Reform and how taxes can change from year to year with new legislation passing through Congress.

We'll end with giving you some insight into the most commonly encountered mistakes that small business owners make when filing their taxes, as well as a frequently asked questions section for your review.

As a business owner, I know first hand that learning about the information you are about to read in this book will help you understand your small business as a whole and in a way that you might not have before.

By knowing how to properly navigate taxation on a small business, you will not only have the peace of mind that you are doing things correctly and can have confidence when it comes time to turn in that return, but you will also reap the benefits by gaining a good credit rating as a business. This is huge, and will show that you and your business are committed to the social responsibility of contributing to the success of your country.

With all of this comes an increase in the chance that your business will be strong and successful.

That all sounds great, right? We have faith that after reading our book, you will truly understand how taxes work, how they apply specifically to your type of small business, and how to lower them so that you can earn more revenue.

If you don't know what you're doing when it comes to taxes as a business owner, you run the risk of harming your business.

What are you waiting for? Buy this book now and become the expert in small business tax that can take their business forward with confidence, and a little extra padding in those pocketbooks.

TAX BASICS

*T*hroughout our lives, we hear about taxes. But what are taxes really? A tax is a fee that is demanded by a government entity on corporations and individuals that is used to finance the government's activities.

In the US, the different types of taxes collected are sales taxes, payroll taxes, real estate taxes and income taxes. Those taxes that are collected get distributed to different agencies within the government, the amounts depending on predetermined budgets.

A great thing about taxes for a small business is that your cost of doing business can be deducted from your revenue every year, thus lowering the amount of tax your business has to pay. But how exactly can you go about that?

There are laws that outline just what specifically you can deduct and what you cannot, as well as the limitations on the amounts that are deductible as well, so it's important to know the ins and outs of tax deduction for your small business. Luckily, you're here reading this book and are about to gain the basic knowledge that you need to make sure your business tax situation is handled correctly.

LET'S GO OVER SOME FREQUENTLY ASKED QUESTIONS REGARDING SOME TAX BASICS FOR A SMALL BUSINESS:

1. What Types Of Taxes Do You Need To Pay?

If you have employees, you will need to pay payroll taxes and make the appropriate contributions into the employees' tax accounts (social security, etc).

If you are selling goods, you'll need to collect the appropriate sales tax for your state and pay those amounts in to the state.

2. Just How Much Do You Have To Pay?

How much you have to pay in taxes will depend on how much your business did in revenue and how much you will be filing for deductions. To estimate your tax, you will need to estimate the amount of income you are expecting to generate for the year, then take away any tax credits or deductions you might be claiming. Then find your tax amount based on that number.

3. When Do You Have To Pay Small Business Taxes?

If your business is a sole-proprietorship or if you are self-employed performing freelance work, you should pay what is called an estimated tax if you are expecting that you will owe over $1000 for the year in taxes. If your business is a corporation, and are expecting to owe over $500 for the year in taxes, you should also pay by estimated tax. Estimated taxes should be filed and paid quarterly. These quarterly payments are due on the 15th of April, June, September and January.

4. How Do You Pay Small Business Taxes?

You can send in quarterly estimated tax payments by:

- Paper check using a Form 1040-ES voucher and mailing it in
- Credit card payment electronically when you enroll in the Electronic Filing Tax Payment System (EFTPS), or use the Direct Pay option.
- The options for electronic payment can be found on the Internal Revenue Service (IRS) website.

WHAT IS TAX CODE AND HOW DOES IT EFFECT HOW THE GOVERNMENT COLLECTS TAXES?

The Tax Code in the US is officially called the Internal Revenue Code (IRC). The IRC is written by Congress and directs the Internal Revenue Service (IRS) in determining how taxes should be collected, how tax refunds, credits and rebates should be issued, and how tax rules should be enforced. The IRS belongs to the US Department of Treasury and is the agency in charge of carrying out all the functions tax-related in the country.

The IRS interprets the tax code through its own regulations that offer guidance on how to properly apply tax law, however, if there is ever a dispute on how a tax code is meant to be executed, the matter goes before a federal court in order to resolve how the code was originally meant to be used when it was written by Congress.

The government collects taxes from individuals by withholdings from paychecks. As a small business, you are responsible for paying in the appropriate amount of tax withholdings from your employees' paychecks. This is called payroll taxation.

Businesses also might pay sales taxes to states at the state's predetermined rate if they have any sales transactions that state tax applies to. When it comes to paying state sales taxes, this varies depending on the state's requirements. Some states just require you to figure the total amount of sales tax you collected during a filing year and pay that amount. Others require that you break down the sales tax you collected by smaller areas such as county or city. Always check to see what your state requires.

Finally, your small business will pay taxes on the final revenue amount for the year. It's common for small businesses to pay estimated taxes in quarterly payments as discussed in the previous section of frequently asked questions.

ACCRUAL ACCOUNTING VERSUS CASH BASIS ACCOUNTING

When you're getting started with a small business, you have to make the decision of what system you want to follow when it comes to accounting. The two types of accounting processes to choose from are Accrual Accounting and Cash Basis Accounting.

Accrual Accounting

Accrual Accounting operates on the basis that revenue and expense are recorded when they are earned, no matter when the money is received or paid.

For example, if your business completed a web design project this month invoiced at $5,000, that $5,000 would go on your books as $5,000 earned for this month. On the flip side, let's also say that your business received a bill for $1,000 for developer fees from work done earlier this same month.

Your books would reflect a profit of $4,000 for this month because you recorded earnings of $5,000 minus the expense of $1,000.

The Accrual Accounting method is required to be used by large corporations that average $25 million or more in gross receipts per year. That being said, it is also recommended by most accountants that you use the Accrual Accounting method if you are a small business or sole proprietorship that carries an inventory.

Pros of Using Accrual Accounting

Some pros of using the Accrual Accounting method for your business are:

- Snapshot of your business over periods of time - When you use Accrual Accounting, you are tracking your income and your expenses by the dates they happen. Doing this can give you a great insight into how your business's money ebbs and flows. You can learn what months are better for business, which ones you spent too much, etc.

- Know how long your customers take to pay - When you track your accounts receivable, you can also get a good glimpse into how long your average client takes to pay off their bill. This is useful information when you want to estimate how much cash you might have on hand at any point in time.

Cons of Using Accrual Accounting

Some cons of using the Accrual Accounting method for your business are:

- Taxes - When you use Accrual Accounting, you have to pay taxes on money that you have yet to receive.

Cash Basis Accounting

With Cash Basis Accounting, revenue is recorded when it is received, and expenses are recorded when they are paid. When you use this method, you do not have an accounts payable (AP) or accounts receivable (AR) to keep track of.

Using the Cash Basis Accounting method, let's say your business received a payment in the amount of $1,000 for a project that was invoiced last month. On the flip side, let's also say that your business paid a bill in the amount of $75 for a utility this month.

Your books would reflect a profit of $925 for this month because you received $1000 in payments and paid out an expense of $75.

The Cash Basis method of accounting is the most commonly used practice for small businesses and sole proprietorships that do not carry an inventory.

Pros of Using Cash Basis Accounting

Some pros of using the Cash Basis method of accounting for your business are:

- Easy to track - With Cash Basis accounting method, you don't have an accounts payable (AP) or accounts receivable (AR) to keep track of. This cuts down on a lot of man hours when it comes to your accounting practices. Things are not recorded until money is received or paid out.
- Quick snapshot of money you have available - Either there is money in the bank or there is not money in the bank.
- You don't pay taxes on money until you receive it.

Cons of Using Cash Basis Accounting

Some cons of using the Cash Basis method of accounting for your business are:

- Not as easy to track actual services billed vs actual expenses owed - Since you're not keeping an AP or AR system, it will be harder for you to see what your actual income was that you generated versus the expenses you accrued each month/quarter/etc.

TAX PREPARATION

Many Americans have turned to using tax software to figure and file their taxes for themselves instead of using a professional. Most software's that are out there currently make filing a step by step seemingly easy process and typically doesn't break the bank, often offering free or low cost packages for filing. But if you don't have a background in tax preparation or advanced tax knowledge, are you short-changing yourself or your business by choosing to trust a software as opposed to the eyes of a trained professional tax preparer?

If you own a business, there are a lot of things to consider when preparing taxes. Tax credits might be out there that you qualify for. That equipment purchase you made a few months ago might qualify as a write-off. It's safe to say, when you own a business, it's likely in your best interest to have a tax professional go over your information and prepare your return. They will know what to look for and how to get you all of the deductions you qualify for.

When choosing a tax professional, it's a wise decision to choose someone who has dealt with your type of business before, and on a regular basis. If they have experience in your particular area of the business world, they will be more qualified to know all the details and ins and outs to look for when perusing your paperwork.

Here are some things to look for when considering a tax preparer:

- Do they have an accounting degree?
- Is tax preparation and accounting their specialty or do they just do it as a side business?
- How long have they been in business/how many years' experience do they have preparing taxes for businesses?
- Do they prepare taxes for your type of business on a regular basis?
- Do they work the entire year or just during the "tax season"?
- Are they an established local business or are they a

pop up that is only open in your area during the tax season?

- Can they tell you up front how much they are going to charge for their services? Or if not an exact amount, can they give you an estimate of the max amount you could be billed?

- Ask them if they will be signing as the "Paid Preparer" on your tax return, claiming responsibility for the information that is reported on the return.

- Ask them how they are prepared to handle audits. They should have a clear plan in place for this.

2

TAXATION AND ACCOUNTING LINGO

*B*efore we go any further into detail, it's important that we go over some common terms that are used in the tax and accounting world. Knowing what these terms mean will help you have a better understanding of what you are reading from here on out.

Terms will be listed in alphabetical order for ease of future reference:

Account

An Account is a record that shows in money, words, or another type of measurement, resources, claims to those resources, and transactions or other happenings that come to cause changes to those claims or resources.

. . .

Accounts Payable

Accounts Payable are goods or services that the business has used or received from a supplier or vendor that the business has an obligation to pay for. It is a liability when keeping a balance sheet. Example: Your business received an invoice for internet service in the amount of $132 for last month. That amount is an expense, and is considered payable. Accounts Payable (sometimes referred to as AP) are tracked when using the Accrual Accounting method.

Accounting Period

An Accounting Period is a time period (typically month, quarter, year) that statements of financial information are prepared.

Accounts Receivable

Accounts Receivable refers to money that is due to a company for goods or services that were supplied to a customer. It is an asset when keeping a balance sheet. Example: Your business completed a marketing project for a customer last week for the cost of $400. That amount is income that is owed to your business, and is considered receivable. Accounts Receivable (sometimes referred to as AR) are tracked when using the Accrual Accounting method.

Accrual Basis

An accounting method that operates on the basis that revenue and expense are recorded when they are earned, no matter when the money is received or paid.

Articles of Organization

The AOC's are part of the legal documentation used for establishing Limited Liability Companies at State level. They are usually filed with a state government.

Assets

An Asset is anything that can be considered of value that is controlled or owned by a business or individual. Assets are something that can be of benefit to the business or individual in the future.

Audit

Audit refers to an examination of a company or individual's financial statements by a professional in order to determine accuracy. Audits can be requested to be completed on any individual or business.

Bad Debt

Bad debt is a form of business expense that incurs when the repayment of credit extended to a customer is now believed to be uncollectible, hence the business may not receive this payment & this must be accounted for, incase the customer does not pay.

Balance Sheet

A financial statement that showcases a company's shareholders' equity, assets & liabilities at a given point in time. It allows for a snapshot of what a company actually owes & owns, as well as total amounts invested by shareholders.

Capital gains taxes

Capital gains taxes are taxes that you pay on whatever your net gains are when you sell assets. Common assets include investments and real estate. You also have to pay tax when you sell collectible or valuable items, such as jewelry or a collection of rare stamps. You pay the long-term capital gains rates, which are lower than the regular tax rates, if you held assets for more than one year. Note that states that collect income tax also collect capital gains taxes.

Federal capital gains rates depend on how long you were the owner of the asset. You pay the short-term capital gains rates if you held assets for one year or less. These rates are the same as regular income tax rates.

* * *

Cash Basis

Cash Basis is an accounting method wThe here revenue is recorded when it is received, and expenses are recorded when they are paid. When you use this method, you do not have an accounts payable (AP) or accounts receivable (AR) to keep track of.

C Corporation

A C corporation is a business recognized as a separate taxpaying entity than just yourself. Corporations have net income or losses, they pay taxes and they distribute any profits to their shareholders.

Commodities

Commodities refer to a bulk of goods like metals, foods, or grains, that are traded on a commodities exchange.

Consumption taxes

Consumption taxes are taxes that are applied when someone purchases certain types of goods or services. These are what is referred to as indirect taxes, because the purchaser is the one paying the tax, but the retailer or supplier of the good or services is responsible for then paying the tax to the government. The two most common types of consumption taxes are value-added tax, and sales tax.

Depreciation

Depreciation is the decrease in value of an asset during its life expectancy.

Employer Identification Number (EIN)

An EIN is a completely unique identification number that is assigned to each and every business entity that is liable to pay taxes, so it can be easily identified by the IRS.

Estate taxes

Estate tax is a tax that is applied to the money and assets that you pass on to others after your death. This can include cash, investments, real estate and other valuables. Your estate pays the tax but how much you pay, if you have to pay anything at all, depends on the value of the estate. Only estates valued above a certain threshold are subject to tax. This threshold is also known as the exemption or exclusion amount. The federal government collects an estate tax, as do 12 states and the District of Columbia. The federal estate tax exemption for 2020 is $11.58 million. This value will increase slightly each year to account for inflation. (In 2019, the estate tax exemption was $11.4 million.) About a dozen states have their own estate tax and exemption amounts vary by state. Some use the same exemption as the federal government. Massachusetts has one of the lowest exemptions, at $1 million.

Most of your assets factor into your estate's value, but note that the death benefit from a life insurance policy does not.

Estimated Taxes

Estimated taxes are down payments on taxes for the current tax year when it's expected that the yearly tax will be greater than $1000. These taxes are typically paid quarterly.

Excise Tax

Excise Tax is the tax on the manufacturing, sale, or use of commodities.

Fiscal Year

A fiscal year is any twelve month period that is used by a business for its accounting period. Fiscal years can be a calendar year, or another twelve-month block determined by a business.

General Partnership

A General Partnership is a partnership that has no limited partners. Partners are equal.

Income Tax

Income taxes are taxes on both earned and unearned income. Examples of earned income are wages, salaries, tips, and commissions. Examples of unearned income are interest or dividends from savings or stocks. Both businesses and individuals are subject to income taxes.

Independent Contractor

Independent contractors are people who do work for a business not actually as an employee. Independent contractors pay self-employment tax. Businesses that contract work with them don't include them on their employment taxes and are not responsible for paying in these types of taxes for them.

Inheritance taxes

Inheritance taxes are applied to whatever is passed on from someone when they die. The person inheriting the assets or money have to pay the tax which is dependent on how much they have just inherited. The tax does not come out of the estate. This tax is at a state level, and currently only six states collect inheritance taxes.

Invoice

Invoice refers to a bill. It is a document that shows a summary of goods or services performed and the cost for each of these items. Invoices often have sale or completion dates, as well as due dates for the cost to be remitted to the business that provided the goods or services.

. . .

Internal Revenue Service (IRS)

The IRS is the corporation responsible for collecting taxes & administering the internal revenue code. Some functions the IRS perform is providing tax assistance to US taxpayers & pursuing and dealing with tax filings that are fraudulent. You don't want to get on their bad side!

Itemized Deductions

Itemized deductions are deductions that can be taken in lieu of the standard deduction on individual income taxes. If all of your deductions will be greater than the amount of the standard deduction, you should itemize to save money.

Liabilities

Liabilities are any debts that a business owes.

Limited Liability

Limited Liability means that the owners of a corporation are not liable for the company's debts, but only for the amount they have invested into the company.

Limited Liability Company (LLC)

Limited Liability Companies are a type of business entity that combines limited liability to all its members (owners) and its taxation is as a partnership. To form a Limited

Liability Company (LLC), you must follow the rules for your state and file the appropriate articles of organization with the correct state official.

Marginal Tax Rates

Marginal Tax Rates are the amount of taxes on an additional dollar of income.

Progressive Taxes

Progressive Taxes are a type of taxation where if you have more income that is subject to tax, you have higher average tax rates. It is called progressive tax because of the fact that as income increases so does the tax rate getting progressively more. Federal income tax brackets use progressive taxation. Graduated income tax is another term used to describe this process as well.

Proportional Taxes

A proportional tax is based on how much have, also known as a flat tax. An example of proportional tax is if you live in a state with a flat income tax of 5%. This means that every taxpayer will pay to the state 5% of their taxable income. Because everyone is paying a 5% proportion of their own income, this is referred to as a proportional tax.

. . .

Regressive Taxes

Regressive taxation is where the more you have the less your tax will be. The opposite of Progressive Taxes. Social Security taxes are an example of a regressive tax. Income up to a certain amount is subject to Social Security taxes, however, the higher the income goes over that limit, the lower the average rate you pay.

S Corporation

In an S Corporation, the taxable income of the corporation is actually passed on to the stockholders of the corporation similar to a partnership. S Corporations are typically not federally taxed according to the Internal Revenue Code (IRC).

Sales tax

A sales tax is a tax that is applied to certain services and goods that you purchase. Sales tax is paid at the time of a sale. States, local district and cities all might have their own determined sales tax rates, while there are no sales taxes at the federal level. Not all states, local districts, and cities collect sales tax, however. Rates may vary depending on what you are purchasing.

.   .   .

Self-Employment Taxes

If you're self-employed, you have to pay the same income and payroll taxes that others pay. But instead of paying the FICA tax, you have to pay self-employment tax. That's a tax equal to 15.3% of your income - 12.4% for Social Security and 2.9% for Medicare.

The good news is that you can deduct 50% of your self-employment taxes when you file your annual income taxes.

Sole Proprietorship

A Sole Proprietorship is a business that is owned by a single person that does not have the protection limited liability of that of a limited liability company (LLC) or a corporation.

Tax Brackets

A Tax Bracket is a system developed by the Internal Revenue Service (IRS) that divides income levels into several groups of ranges. These ranges of income levels are called Tax Brackets. A different tax rate is assigned to each Tax Bracket.

Tax Deductions

Tax Deductions are certain expenses that you incur during your tax year that the government will allow you to take away from your taxable income. Tax Deductions are available for both individuals and businesses.

Tax Year

Tax Years are twelve consecutive months that determine a time bracket for taxes and income reporting. Tax Years could follow a calendar year of January to December, or they could follow a fiscal year determined by a company. A fiscal year can be twelve consecutive months other than January to December. For example, July 1st - June 30th could be considered a chosen fiscal year for a company to use.

Value-added tax

A value-added tax (VAT) applies to goods that are purchased and is added in to a retail price already because the product was already taxed throughout production. The tax is added at each different stage of production because each stage adds value to the product as it is being made.

Withholding Allowance

A Withholding Allowance is something a taxpayer can claim that will exempt a portion of their earnings from being subject to withholding.

3

TAXES AND BUSINESS ENTITIES

TAXES WE PAY AS INDIVIDUALS

Federal income tax

Income tax is defined as a tax that is applied to your income, wages and earnings. The federal government uses a tax with seven marginal tax rates that is what is known as a progressive tax. It collects tax over the course of the year. For most people, tax comes out of your paycheck. If you are self-employed or a freelancer, you will probably need to make estimated tax payments each quarter. In a perfect world, you would pay the exact amount in tax that you need to, but since many people overpay, they receive a tax refund each year.

Local And State Income Taxes

Most states also have an income tax. Only seven states do not have an income tax:

- Alaska - no income tax
- Florida- no income tax
- Nevada- no income tax
- South Dakota- no income tax
- Texas- no income tax
- Washington- no income tax
- Wyoming- no income tax
- New Hampshire - does not tax most regular income but do tax income from interest and dividends.
- Tennessee - does not tax most regular income but do tax income from interest and dividends. (Note that Tennessee's tax on investment income will expire in 2022.)

Nine states have a flat tax rate:

- Colorado - flat tax rate
- Illinois - flat tax rate
- Indiana - flat tax rate
- Kentucky - flat tax rate
- Massachusetts - flat tax rate
- Michigan - flat tax rate

- North Carolina - flat tax rate
- Pennsylvania - flat tax rate
- Utah - flat tax rate

The rest of the states in the US use marginal tax brackets. However, the number of brackets and the income ranges within each bracket differ from state to state.

For example:

Alabama has tax rates of 2%, 4% and 5% depending on your income. Some cities, counties and local governments also collect income taxes. In the state of Missouri, the cities of Kansas City and St. Louis collect an income tax. In the state of Oregon, the cities in the Portland area have a special income tax that supports public transit. In the state of Maryland, each county has its own income tax that is collected.

FICA And Payroll Taxes

These are taxes that employers remove from your paycheck and send to the appropriate government agency. If you're a freelancer or self-employed, you will need to pay these on a quarterly basis via estimated taxes.

In addition to income taxes, there are federal taxes that fund Social Security and Medicare. These together are the FICA (Federal Insurance Contributions Act) taxes. Taxpayers need to pay 6.2% of their income to Social Security and 1.45% to

Medicare. Your employer also contributes an equal amount of FICA tax for you.

There is an additional Medicare surtax of 0.9% for single filers who earn more than $200,000 and joint filers who earn more than $250,000. This tax, called the Additional Medicare Tax, applies only to income above those thresholds.

There are five different types of business entities and they all have differences when it comes to taxes and taxation processes.

The five types of business entities are Sole Proprietorship, General Partnership, Limited Liability, C Corporation, and S Corporation.

To look at these business entities comparatively, let's look at the chart below. You will be able to see each type of business entity, the number of owners allowed for each type, if they have limited liability, if they use a pass-through tax, and what tax forms are necessary for each entity as well.

BUSINESS ENTITY TYPE	NUMBER OF OWNERS	LIMITED LIABILITY	PASS-THROUGH TAX	TAX FORMS
Sole Proprietorship	1	No	Yes	Schedule C or Schedule C-EZ to Form 1040, Individual Income Tax Return
General Partnership	2 or more	No	Yes	Form 1065, US Return of Partnership Income
Limited Liability	1 or more	Yes	Yes	Form 8832 or Form 1120S. OR Schedule C, Schedule E, or Schedule F to Form 1040 or 1040-SR Individual Income Tax Return
C Corporation	Unlimited	No	No	Form 1120, US Corporation Income Tax Return
S Corporation	Max of 100	No	No	Form 1120S, 1120S(Sch.K-1)

There are of course advantages and disadvantages to each type of business entity. If you're just forming your company, you'll want to take into consideration the pros and cons for each in order to decide which type of business entity best suits you and what you, any partners or investors you have, and what you are looking for in a business.

Sole Proprietorship

Sole proprietorships are the simplest business structure that there is. It includes just one owner who is solely responsible for how the business runs, the profits and losses of the business, and the legalities and liabilities of the business.

There is no legal paperwork required to start a sole-proprietorship.

* * *

Advantages:

- Sole Proprietors don't have to do anything but start operating in order to start their business. There is no extra setup included because they are the sole owner.
- Being the sole proprietor means that all of the money made and all of the control are in the hands of only the sole proprietor. No divvying up profits, sharing control of business decisions, etc.
- Sole Proprietors do not have to file business income taxes. Their business income is reported on their individual tax returns.

Disadvantages:

- Sole proprietors are held responsible on a personal level for any and all debts that their business may incur. This means that debt collectors can come after a sole proprietor's personal savings, assets, and property if the business accounts aren't able to pay for a debt.
- If for some reason a sole-proprietor wishes to add a co-owner to their business, they have to dissolve the sole-proprietorship in order to do so.

General Partnership

A General Partnership is a partnership that has no limited partners. In a general partnership, two or more partners are equal at sharing the profits and losses of the business, as well as the legalities and liabilities.

Advantages:

- With a partner, upon creating the business you not only have their help, but you also start off with twice the connections as you would have on your own.
- General partnerships are easy to create. Technically all you need to do to form a general partnership is to have a partner and work together to make an income.
- General partnerships are simple for taxes because the partners' individual incomes from the business are taxed on their individual tax returns, and not on separate business taxes.
- When in a general partnership, you and your partner are the ones who decide who is in charge of what part of the business, how to split up profit and loss, etc.

Disadvantages:

- In a partnership, you are liable for your partner's decisions, and vice versa. These decisions can affect the other's profits and losses, and how they interact with the running of the business.
- Both partners are personally liable for any business debt incurred and any legal issues that might affect the business. This means that debt collectors can come after both partners on a personal level for business debt, including personal savings, assets, and property if the business accounts aren't able to pay for a debt.

Limited Liability

Limited Liability Companies are a type of business entity that combines limited liability to all its members (owners) and its taxation is as a partnership. To form a Limited Liability Company (LLC), you must follow the rules for your state and file the appropriate articles of organization with the correct state official.

Advantages:

- With an LLC, there is no restriction on the number of members that are allowed

- There are fewer restrictions and formalities involved with an LLC as there are in a corporation.
- When you have an LLC, as an owner you are protected and are not held responsible on a personal level for business debts or legalities.
- The members of an LLC are able to form the company and its structure and functions as they choose to.
- An LLC can be managed by its members or managed by a dedicated manager.
- Limited Liability Companies use pass-through taxation. This means that any profit or loss passes through the business to its members. Members report the profit and losses on their own individual tax returns.
- Any kind of LLC can file taxes as an S Corporation or C Corporation if they choose to do so.

Disadvantages:

- Both salaries and profits of an LLC are subject to self-employment taxes.
- Some states charge extra fees when you operate an LLC, and limit certain types of groups from forming an LLC (i.e. doctors, dentists, etc.).

C Corporation

A C corporation is a business recognized as a separate taxpaying entity than just yourself. Corporations have net income or losses; they pay taxes and they distribute any profits to their shareholders.

Advantages:

- Owners are protected from being personally liable for business legalities, liabilities and debts.
- C Corporations are able to have an unlimited number of owners.
- A corporation has an easier time in general gaining the attention of investors. People would rather own shares in a corporation than owning membership in an LLC for example.
- Corporations exist until they are dismantled or dissolved, as compared with a sole-proprietorship that would cease to exist if the owner dies.

Disadvantages:

- Subject to double taxation because this type of business pays taxes at a corporate level.
- A C Corporation has many more complex issues to deal with when it comes to general operation and

taxation. Corporate law has strict tax record keeping requirements.

S Corporation

In an S Corporation, the taxable income of the corporation is actually passed on to the stockholders of the corporation similar to a partnership. S Corporations are typically not federally taxed according to the Internal Revenue Code (IRC).

Advantages:

- Owners are protected from being personally liable for business legalities, liabilities and debts.
- Not subject to double taxation. Unlike a C Corporation, an S Corporation uses pass-through taxation. This means that any profit or loss passes through the business to its shareholders. Shareholders report the profit and losses on their own individual tax returns.
- S Corporation shareholders are allowed to be employees of the business and take salaries.
- Ownership interest can be transferred or sold without risking the integrity of the business.

Disadvantages:

- An S Corporation has many more complex issues to deal with when it comes to general operation and taxation. It must follow the struct tax record keeping requirements and rules and regulations under corporate law.

- S Corporations typically have to follow a calendar year for tax purposes unless they can come up with a reason that will affect the operations of the business as to why they need to adopt a fiscal year.

- If there are mistakes made regarding stock ownerships, filing requirements, or certain elections, consents or notifications, this can result in the termination of the S Corporation status. S Corporations are the only type of business that deals with this as a factor.

4

INTERNAL REVENUE SERVICE

IRS FACTS

*T*he Internal Revenue Service (IRS) is the government agency under the US Department of Treasury that is in charge of all things taxes and applying and executing the tax code. Its main function is to collect employment taxes and individual taxes.

The IRS was established by President Abraham Lincoln clear back in 1862. Its headquarters are in Washington, D.C. Just to give you an idea on the scope of work the IRS does, it processed more than 250 million income tax returns and forms for the 2019 fiscal year. For that sole fiscal year, $3.5 trillion in revenue was collected by the IRS, and $452 billion in tax refunds were issued by the IRS.

You've probably heard people complain that the IRS is slow, they are waiting on their tax returns to be processed, it's taking forever... but when you have the information above, you might want to think again and consider the grand scheme of work that is being done. While some would argue there is room for improvement, in reality, returns are processed much faster now than they used to be.

Thanks to modern technology, close to 90% of all tax returns are filed to the IRS electronically. Electronic filing speeds the process for the IRS and all involved.

In addition to handling income and employment tax, the IRS also handles corporate tax, gift tax, excise and estate taxes, mutual funds and dividends.

TAXPAYERS BILL OF RIGHTS

The IRS has put into place a Taxpayer's Bill Of Rights. This bill of rights groups the rights in the tax code into ten rights, and attempts to make them clear so that all taxpayers can understand and access them in order to know their rights.

The ten rights included in the Taxpayer's Bill of Rights are:

1. The Right To Be Informed

Taxpayers have the right to know how to comply with tax laws and what they should to in order to do so. They are entitled to what is deemed as a clear explanation of the laws, as well as the IRS procedures in all tax forms, instructions and their publications, as well as any notices and correspondence that might be sent or posted. They have the right to be kept up on the decisions made by the IRS about their own tax accounts and to get clear explanations of their outcomes.

Some specific ways this might apply to you include:

- If you are being audited, the person conducting the audit must explain your rights and the process to you.
- If you owe a penalty amount, the IRS has to always state an explanation of the penalty including the specific name of the penalty and how it has been calculated.
- If your refund claim has been disallowed either partially or fully, the IRS has to explain why.
- If the amount of tax you owe is being adjusted, they have to send you a notification of this proposed change and you have the right to challenge it in Tax Court.

2. The Right To Quality Service

Taxpayers have the right to receive timely, courteous, and professional service and help when they have to communicate with the IRS. The service that they receive from the IRS should include information that is clear and easy to understand. They also have the right to have a way to lodge a complaint if they feel they have received service that doesn't uphold these standards.

Some specific ways this might apply to you include:

- The IRS should always be courteous and only contact you during the hours of 8am and 9pm.
- Some notices from the IRS are required to include the information of the employee that is initiating the contact via the notice including a phone number so the taxpayer can contact them.

3. The Right To Pay The Correct Amount of Tax

Taxpayers have the right to only need to pay the amount of tax that is legally due, and the IRS has a duty to apply all tax payments that they receive in a proper manner.

Some specific ways this might apply to you include:

- If you think you overpaid on your taxes, you are able to file a refund claim as long as you adhere to time limitations.
- You can request that any amount that is showing as

owed by you or your business be removed if it's incorrect.

- You can request that the IRS remove fees for interest if the fees were incurred during a time when the IRS caused an unreasonable delay in process.

4. The Right To Challenge The IRS's Position And Be Heard

Taxpayers have the right to object to and give more documentation in response to any formal IRS actions or proposed actions. They also should expect that the IRS will take their objections into consideration as long as they were turned in timely and fairly, and should expect a response if the IRS doesn't agree with their position.

Some specific ways this might apply to you include:

- If you think the IRS made a clerical or mathematical error, you have the right to tell the IRS you disagree with them within 60 days. If they do not agree, you have the right to request the matter be reviewed in Tax Court.
- If the IRS plans to collect any outstanding tax debt owed by you by levying your bank account, you have

the right to a hearing in front of an independent appeals or settlement officer. You will be able to suggest alternatives to the planned levying, and also have the opportunity to challenge whether or not you owe the debt if that is in question.

5. The Right To Appeal An IRS Decision In An Independent Forum

Taxpayers are allowed to have a fair and impartial administrative appeal when it comes to most of the IRS decisions. These include many penalties, and the taxpayers have the right to receive responses about the Office of Appeals' decision in writing. In general, taxpayers also have the right to decide their case should be taken to court.

Some specific ways this might apply to you include:

- For some situations, you have the right to request a conference with the Office Of Appeals.
- The IRS has to make sure that an appeals officer is available in every state.
- If you don't agree with any adjustments that result from an audit, you have the right to administrative appeal.

6. The Right To Finality

Taxpayers have the right to be informed of what the maximum amount of time is that they are allowed to challenge the IRS's position, as well as the limitations on the time the IRS has to audit any given tax year. Taxpayers also have the right to be informed when the IRS has completed an audit.

Some specific ways this might apply to you include:

- The IRS typically has ten years to collect unpaid taxes. Certain circumstances might result in the ten-year period being suspended.
- Generally, you are only subject to one audit per financial year.
- If you are being charged additional tax for some reason, the notification of such must give you a deadline to challenge that amount in Tax Court.

7. The Right To Privacy

Taxpayers have the right to believe and expect that the IRS will comply with the law, will not be any more intrusive than necessary, when conducting inquiries, examinations, and enforcement actions. They will also respect due process rights which include search and seizure protections and a due process hearing for collections when it is applicable.

Some specific ways this might apply to you include:

- If the IRS seizes and sells your property, they have to provide you with a breakdown of how they applied the monies received for such to your debt.
- During audits, the IRS cannot and should not seek out intrusive and irrelevant information about you and your life if it doesn't apply to indicating there is unreported income.

8. The Right To Confidentiality

Taxpayers have the right to count on any information that is given to the IRS provide to will not be disclosed to anyone unless they, the taxpayer, has authorized it by law. Taxpayers also have the right to expect the IRS will proceed with investigation and take necessary action against its employees, preparers of returns, and anyone else who wrongfully uses or discloses the taxpayer's return information.

Some specific ways this might apply to you include:

- The IRS cannot and will not disclose your personal info to third parties with your express permission.
- Tax preparers cannot and will not disclose your personal information to third parties for any

purpose other than preparing your taxes. They are
subject to penalty under law for doing so.

- The IRS can't contact third parties about collecting
your owed taxes unless it gives you what is
considered reasonable advance notice.

9. The Right To Retain Representation

Taxpayers have the right to have an authorized representative of their choosing that can represent them when they are
needing to deal with the IRS. Taxpayers also have the right
to be informed that there is legal assistance possibly available
to them from a Low-Income Taxpayer Clinic if they can't
afford to pay for a representative themselves.

Some specific ways this might apply to you include:

- If you go to court and win your case, you may be
entitled to administrative and legal costs related to
your case.
- The IRS must stop an interview in most cases if
you request to have legal representation present.
- You can have a legal representative represent you
for an IRS interview (attorney, accountant, etc.).

10. The Right To A Fair And Just Tax System

Taxpayers have the right to count on facts and circumstances being considered by the tax system when it might affect their liabilities, ability to pay, or ability to give necessary information in a timely manner. Taxpayers also have the right to be given assistance from the Taxpayer Advocate Service when they are having financial difficulties, or if normal channels the IRS uses have not solved their tax issues in a proper and timely manner.

Some specific ways this might apply to you include:

- If you are suffering from physical or mental health issues, the time limit for taxes you paid being refunded might be suspended if you aren't able to manage your own affairs.
- If your tax preparer is found to have been reckless when completing your taxes in regards to reporting, they are subject to being penalized.
- There are steps you can take to be helped by an advocate service if the tax debt you owe is causing a hardship.
- The IRS should consider your income, assets, and expenses when working out a compromise for your tax debt repayment plan.

STATUTE OF LIMITATIONS

You've likely heard the term statute of limitations before, but do you really know what it means? A statute of limitations is actually a law that sets the maximum time that parties have to initiate legal proceedings.

Statutes of limitations apply to both criminal and civil law, however, the amount of time a statute of limitation allows a victim to move ahead with legal action against the person or entity who is suspected of the wrong-doing can vary in different jurisdictions, as well as by the type of offense that has supposedly been committed.

An example of a civil case would be if someone believes they were injured wrongfully as a direct result of a surgery error, and the statute of limitations for that type of case in their jurisdiction was two years, they would have two years from the date of the surgery to file a case. If they waited for just one day past that two-year deadline, they would not be able to file.

The statute would work the same way for a criminal case, again depending on the length of the statute for the particular type of case in the jurisdiction where the crime was supposedly committed. There are exceptions to this rule, however. Many cases involving serious crimes usually have no max period of statute of limitations. Some examples of such types of crimes are murder, sex offenses involving minors, arson, and kidnapping.

With international law, war crimes, genocide, and crimes against humanity join the list of serious crimes that have no statute of limitations.

So, now that you know what this term means and how it applies in general, how does it apply to taxes? This brings us to the subject of audits.

IRS AUDITS

The IRS typically has a statute of limitations of three years from the filing due date of a tax year to engage in an audit. However, there are a few reasons why they can go beyond that statute:

- The statute of limitations is automatically lengthened to six years if you the IRS believes that your return has a "substantial understatement of income". Basically, this means that they have reason to believe you have left off at least 25% of your annual gross income. You could have just made an error on your income reporting. Or you for some reason didn't believe that 25% you left off was actually your income. Regardless, the IRS can audit you anytime from six years of the due date of the year in question's filing for this.

- Foreign income, assets, and foreign gifts are another thing that if underreported by more than $5,000, can double the statute of limitations to six years again. Offshore accounts are of big interest for the IRS nowadays. You'll want to make sure if you have one, you include it in your taxes. Gifts or inheritances from a foreign individual require a certain form to be filed to claim it if it was over $100,000.

- If you don't file a return, or if your return was considered fraudulent, the statute of limitations can never begin on that return which means the IRS can audit for that year indefinitely. Some reasons a return might be considered fraudulent or if it would not be accepted are altering the penalties of perjury section at the bottom of the return, not signing the return, or forgetting to turn in a required form.

If you are being audited and you are confident that the IRS is acting outside the statute of limitations, you have the right to say so. However, they may have a reason such as the ones listed above that allows them to carry on.

THE TEN THINGS YOU SHOULD DO WHEN FACING AN IRS AUDIT

1. **Do Not Ignore Your Auditor** - Ignoring an audit by the IRS is quite possibly the worst thing you can do after finding out that you are being audited. The IRS does not need you to respond in order to proceed with the audit and they will not wait if you refuse to do so. If they move forward without your assistance, contacting third parties to get the information that they need to proceed, including but not limited to bank statements, information from vendors and suppliers, etc. An audit is not going to go away just because you're pretending like it's not happening. Do yourself a favor and cooperate with the process.

2. **Be Honest** - IRS Auditors are federal agents. That means it's a crime to lie to them. If for some reason you feel like you need to lie, don't do it! Be honest with what you say to the auditor and what you supply to them.

3. **Exercise Your Right To Appeal** - An Auditor's word is not gold. You do have the right to appeal with the IRS Office of Appeals if you disagree with facts that have been presented of how

the tax law has been applied in your situation. If you file an appeal, you will have a chance to plead your case with an appeals officer, who basically will give a second opinion on the case. If you don't agree with the appeals officer, you can take your case to tax court.

4. **Get Your Past-Due Tax Returns Filed Immediately** - If you have past-due tax returns, get them filed right away. During an audit, your auditor will review at least the last six years of your filings and returns. Not getting your past-due returns filed will not bring your audit to a screeching halt, so don't even think about using that as a tactic. The IRS auditor can file your past-due returns for you. This is called a substitute return, and it will include nothing in the way of deductions, credits or dependents.

5. **Be Prepared** - If you are not prepared for your audit, the auditor is not going to just take your word for things. You will need to show them what they need to see, and if you don't have things ready for them, it's likely they will want to see more than they would have if you'd laid things out for them right away. If they think there is a problem unfolding, they might ask for other years that weren't previously included. If you own a business,

it's a good practice to hold a mock-audit for practice so that when one actually happens, you are prepared and know how to get the auditor what they need.

6. **Know When To Ask For Their Manager -** If you feel like your audit is taking too long and no progress is being made, you have the right to ask to speak with your auditor's manager. It's actually a good idea to get the auditor's contact information as well as their manager's information at the very start of the auditing process so that if any issues arise you can contact the necessary party. If there is a disagreement between yourself and the auditor, go to the manager first instead of proceeding and waiting to appeal after the whole audit is finished.

7. **Ask For Information Requests In Writing -** It's a good rule of thumb to ask your auditor to provide you with a written or typed list of all of the information they are requiring you to present. Any communications and responses should also be put into writing even if they were face to face. This will get rid of the chance for confusion on both parties parts and will allow you both to focus on the specific issues that you need to. You will also have a written record of facts that are readily available if

for some reason you need to go to a manager, or file an appeal and go to tax court.

8. **Keep Track Of Your Deadlines** - You're a business person, so hopefully keeping track of deadlines is not something that is new to you. In order to run a successful business, you need to keep track of and meet deadlines. This is no different with an audit process. During the course of your audit, there will be many deadlines that you will need to keep track of and meet. An initial appointment, deadlines to give them information that they require, deadlines to respond to their initial report following audit, deadlines to contact the IRS for appeal, deadlines to contact appeal for tax court, etc. Just like you will have deadlines during this audit process, your auditors will also have deadlines that they need to meet. In general, auditors like to have cases closed within two years after a return is filed.

9. **Examine Facts For Unnecessary Penalties** - You should always examine the facts in your situation and check for any unnecessary penalties that were applied by your auditor. If this happens, you will need to be ready to explain why the penalty doesn't apply to you or your business and prove to the IRS that it is an error. Remember, go

to the auditor's manager first before the audit is complete, and then any problems noticed after, go to the IRS appeals and then tax court.

10. **Seek The Help Of A Tax Professional -**

When you speak to auditors about your situation in a face to face audit, you need to know your rights as a taxpayer, as well as know the ins and outs of an audit and how to speak up on your own behalf. If you aren't a trained tax professional, you should probably have one helping you during an audit. It will cost you money, but it will be money well spent in the long run. Typically for a normal audit, a tax professional could spend a few days preparing for you, then meeting with the IRS auditor and getting things wrapped up and finalized. The time it takes for the process will be longer if there are multiple years involved in the audit. The tax professional that you choose should be able to give you an idea of what their fees will be up front so you know what to expect.

5

RECORD-KEEPING AND GOOD STANDING

K eeping accurate records is quite possibly the most important thing you can do for yourself and your business. Tax record keeping in particular is the most important type of record keeping that should be kept in tip top shape consistently at all times.

There are many types of records a business needs to keep track of. The most common records a business tracks include:

- Business bank statements
- Financial statements
- Purchase receipts
- Customer invoicing
- Names of employees and their general contact information such as address and phone number

- Employee timesheets
- Employee pay stubs
- Tax returns for the business
- All tax forms that have been submitted to the IRS
- Insurance documentation
- Contracts, including mortgages and loans
- Business registration documents
- Legal information
- Important meeting minutes
- Important Emails

Some tips on having a good tax record keeping practice include the following.

EMPLOYEE PAYROLL TAX DEDUCTIONS

Keeping a good record of the complexities that come with employee payroll tax deductions is of the utmost importance not only for your business but for your employees' sake as well. You need to make sure that you have record of everything you do in regards to this subject. It is also necessary to keep up on the reporting that is required and deposit payroll taxes regularly and on time.

These reporting requirements include: Wage and Tax Statements (W2s), Employer's Quarterly Payroll Tax Return

(Form 941), Annual Return of Withheld Federal Income Tax (Form 945), Make your federal tax deposits, Annual Federal Unemployment Tax Return (Form 940 or Form 940EZ)

HAVE A GOOD ACCOUNTING SYSTEM IN PLACE

Part of a good accounting system is accounting software that fits the needs of your business. If you want your tax records to be complete and accurate and easy to access, you need accounting software. Another part of your accounting system should be a tax professional that can prepare your taxes for you using the information you provide them. Accounting software that has been kept up and has accurate info will result in your business having accurate tax returns being filed.

BURDEN OF PROOF

When you make an entry (e.g., income, expenses, and deductions) on your tax return, you have what is known as the burden of proof. You must be able to prove that you are entitled to certain deductions and expenses to be eligible to claim them.

. . .

How do you establish proof?

Through good record keeping. If you have records substantiating those deductions and expenses, you have satisfied the burden of proof for the IRS. Do not take any deductions or claim any income if you don't have the documentation to show as proof of them if asked.

Original Documentation

The original documents for purchases (receipts, canceled checks, etc.) should be used to create entries into your record keeping logs or journals. Original documentation is also your proof that you qualify for certain tax deductions. If you can't prove you had the expense, you can't claim it as a deduction, so keep those receipts!

Keep the originals with your logs and ledgers of transactions. It's a good practice to scan all original documentation onto a computer or store them on a flash drive in case of fire or natural disaster.

As much as they'd love to take your word for it, the IRS requires that you keep documentation that backs up the income, deductions, and credits you report on your tax return.

Let's go through a quick list of the main types of records you should keep for your business:

- Receipts
- Cash register tapes
- Deposit information (cash and credit sales)
- Invoices
- Canceled checks or other proof of payment/electronic funds transferred
- Credit card receipts
- Bank statements
- Petty cash slips for small cash payments
- Accounts payable and receivable
- Payroll records
- Tax filings
- Previous tax returns
- W2 and 1099 forms
- Any other document that can serve as evidence for an income, a deduction, or a credit that is going to be shown on your tax return

Payments and Electronic Funds Transfers (EFTs)

With the advancements in modern technology at our fingertips, not only as consumers but as business owners as well, we have electronic transactions to keep track of as well as paper ones. Likely your electronic and online dealings are far more prevalent than paper and cash anymore.

Using credit cards, debit cards, and electronic funds transfers (EFTs) to pay for bills and business expenses. Use your bank statements and credit card statements along with your original documentation (receipts, etc.) to reconcile transactions.

Make sure that EFT statements include the amount of the transfer, the payee's name, and the date the transfer posted to the account. Credit cards should show the same info, but should also include the date of the transaction as well.

Tax deductions could be hiding within all of this documentation as well, so keep up on it and keep it accurate!

SUMMARIES OF CASH RECEIVED AND PAYMENTS DISPERSED

Daily cash receipts and cash disbursements should be logged daily. Don't wait to do it next week or next month. Keep track each day. At the end of each month, keep a monthly log of cash receipts and cash disbursements as well.

If you are needing to find record of a transaction, these types of records will be a god-send when all else fails. Remember to include original documentation (receipts, invoices, deposit tickets, cancelled checks, etc.).

PETTY CASH

Keeping track of your petty cash is necessary. Make sure that purchases are logged and that receipts are logged as well. Some petty cash purchases or disbursements may be tax-deductible, so make sure you are turning over your petty cash records to your tax pro for review as well.

HOW LONG DO YOU NEED TO KEEP RECORDS?

The Internal Revenue Tax Code requires that you keep records as long as they might be needed in order to administer any part of the tax code. Businesses that have employees have to keep their records for at least 4 years. It is recommended that employee records should be kept for at least 7 years.

If you owe taxes, you should keep your records for a minimum of 3 years. If you own any properties, you should keep records that are associated with those properties until the period of limitations expires for the year you no longer have the property. If you have income that is reportable but haven't reported it, and it's more than 25% of the gross income on a tax return, you should keep records for at least 6 years.

It may seem like it makes sense to keep records for as long as you have the space to, but you are permitted to delete records that haven't been relevant in your business if they are more than seven years old.

By downsizing your pile of records, you're making it easier to search for and review documents you actually need. Imagine how much lighter those cabinets will be, or how much space you can free up in your documents on your PC. But before you go about purging your records, consider if others in the business may still need them for one reason or another. Check with a legal professional before you go about erasing or throwing away a large amount of business documents. There may be good reasons to keep them.

TIPS FOR RECORD KEEPING IN YOUR SMALL BUSINESS

Here are some helpful tips to consider when it comes to keeping records for your small business.

1. **Keep your personal records completely separate from your business records.** This will be most challenging for those who own a sole proprietorship; however, general partnerships and LLCs will too have this as an issue at least in a small

way. Everything that is related to the business should be kept in its own record system, and money for the business should be kept separate from personal money accounts. Having a separate bank account or accounts for your small business is especially helpful so that you aren't confusing funds and you know what your business's financial health is like at any given time.

2. **Set aside money to pay your quarterly taxes.** If you are paying estimated taxes, they are due quarterly, and it's a good practice to set aside some money each month to go towards your quarterly tax payment. That way if something happens and you have a short month, you've already gotten the taxes in for previous months and it won't be so hard to catch it up, or even worse, try to pull together the entirely quarterly amount at the last minute when it is due. Things can happen and when it comes time to pay, you don't want to come up short or be empty handed.

3. **Have an organizational system in place for all of your documentation.** Maybe you're groaning and grumbling about how much you hate filing, or how you'll remember where you stored that file on your PC. Take it from us when we say

that having a system is important, and actually following and using that system is possibly the most important favor you can do for you and your business. Two main reasons to have a system and use it are that when you need to find something, you can, and easily, and second, you have everything up to date and, in its place, if you ever have to go through an audit. You should have a system for paper documentation, your electronic documentation that is stored on your hard-drive, and any online documentation that needs to be stored.

4. **Keep a good track of cash.** Cash payments made to your business should be logged into your books under whatever type of transaction they should be, and then deposited into the business bank account before that money is used for anything else. While it might be tempting to grab cash from the cash drawer to use to pay a supplier that shows up with a shipment, don't do it! It will wreak havoc on making sense of your books later on. And it can be especially embarrassing if that cash came from a customer and the payment didn't get logged onto their account. They will wonder why they are getting an invoice for something that they already paid.

5. **Send invoices in a timely manner.** Speaking of invoices, make sure that you send out invoices for any amounts due to your business in a timely manner and regularly. Your customers will appreciate getting a bill so they know how much they owe, and you'll appreciate getting your payments faster. You don't want to look disorganized to your customers by not sending out bills. Invoicing should only apply to businesses that are not operating on a cash basis since with that type of business, you are getting the amount due at the time of the sale.

6. **Pay Employees On Time.** Never ever, ever miss a payroll. This is an unacceptable event as a business owner. If you cannot afford to pay your employees, they should not be working. They rely on their paychecks to be able to eat, pay their housing and live. You also need to set aside and pay in the appropriate amounts for their taxes as well.

7. **Digitize. The easiest way to keep records is to digitize them.** According to the IRS, as long as you can show your income and expenses in a clear and precise way, you can use any type of recordkeeping system. This means, you can go paperless if you choose to do so. That means instead of having filing cabinets full of receipts, you can

simply scan those receipts and save them on a hard drive or dedicated server, etc, and have your "filing cabinets" be virtual. Going paperless is okay with the IRS as long as you can provide them with a legible copy of whatever documentation they request from you. So, if you do scan, make sure the scan is a good one before throwing away that original receipt. Digitizing is a great way to never have the problem of trying to find a box of receipts that should have been filed, or losing them to a flooded basement or a fire. When you digitize, you can save something in your archives and have it forever at your fingertips.

FILING SYSTEMS

Paper-Based

Sometimes we don't need all the bells and whistles and sticking to the simple systems might work best for you and your company. If that is the case and you'll be using a paper-based filing system, here are some tools you can use to help your organization along the way.

File Folder

File folders hold loose papers together in order to keep them protected and organized. They are available at supply stores and big box stores alike. Labels can be purchased or you can write on the tabs of the folders directly so that you can easily see what is in each file folder. Keep like items together in order to aid the ease of your system.

Filing Cabinets

If you are using file folders and keeping paper, you'll definitely need some file cabinets to keep those records in. There are lots of different sizes, shapes and styles of filing cabinets so you'll want to take a look at what is out there and choose what will work best for the type of documentation you'll be filing, as well as the system you will be using. Another tip about filing cabinets and business documents is that you should keep them locked.

Hanging Folder

When you use hanging folders, you can keep several file folders together of like documents in a group. A hanging folder may be labeled "Clients" if it holds a number of individual folders of clients.

Accordion Folder

Accordion folders open like an accordion, hence, their name. They open at the top and fold out to reveal multiple compartments for storage. Basically, an accordion folder is a filing cabinet without the cabinet. They should be stored on a shelf or someplace where they can't fall over and spill or have the contents disturbed. If you're using these, always close them up again!

Electronic Based

If you decide to keep your records mostly electronically, there are several different tips and tricks you can use to manage records electronically.

Bookkeeping Software

Invest in some good bookkeeping software that includes storage of documents. Not only is bookkeeping software a good way to keep track of your financials for your business on all levels, it can also help you keep your records organized.

Electronic client accounts that show incoming and outgoing transactions, invoices, general information. You might also be able to scan in any paper documentation that needs to be stored for your client accounts as well.

Tax information, timecards, employee records, etc. Even if you end up with a couple of different programs that do separate things, you should be able to find a solution or solutions that work for you and your business.

Scanning

When you own a business, you will always have paper documentation that needs to be saved. But if you've elected to go with electronic based record keeping, you'll want to invest in a good scanner that will allow you to scan documents into a PC or onto a server for safe storage.

Electronic File Organization

If you're using electronic filing, you'll want to set up a system to keep all of those electronic files organized on your computer or server, or wherever you have decided to save them. A good suggestion here is to start with a base folder. Think of your base folder as your 'filing cabinet'. What all like items do you want to keep in that filing cabinet? Maybe you want base folders for taxes, employee records, clients, etc. Then within each of those base folders, create subfolders that you can branch off that would be more specific sections of info.

An example would be:

```
Base Folder - Taxes
    Subfolder 1 - 2019
            Folder - Tax Returns
            Folder - Tax Bills And Statements
            Folder - Employee Withholding
            Folder - 1099s
    Subfolder 2 - 2020
            Folder - Tax Returns
            Folder - Tax Bills And Statements
            Folder - Employee Withholding
            Folder - 1099s
```

And so on.

How Long Should I Keep Stuff?

Below, let us give you an example of a business record retention schedule. Please note that when considering a retention schedule, you'll want to make sure that whatever you choose lands on what is needed for your specific type of business.

Accounting and Fiscal Records:

Invoices and receivables - 5 years

Payables and Checks - 5 years

Auditor reports - permanently

Annual statements of any kind - permanently

Inventory record - 4 years

Personnel Records:

Personnel files - 3 years

Contracts - 4-5 years

Insurance Records - 5 years

Timecards or Timesheets - 2 years

Retirement plan documentation - permanently

Business and Corporate Records:

Contracts - 7 years

Copyright Documents - Permanently

Business Correspondence - 3 years

Business Leases - 6 years

Property records - permanently

Customer records - Depends on your type of business

Sales records - Depends on your type of business

Licenses and permits - as required by state and your business type

Insurance policies - as required by state and business type

Tax Records and Documents:

Tax returns - permanently

Employee withholding documentation - 7 years

Tax bills and statements - permanently

1099 form for contractor or nonemployee compensation - permanently

If you ever have a situation where someone has threatened to sue you or your business, you should discuss immediately with your attorney what records you should keep just in case you are drawn into litigation.

Involve Yourself In Bookkeeping Checks

If you own a small business and have a bookkeeper, you probably have faith that this person knows what they are doing and is doing their job efficiently, regularly, and in a timely manner, and that they are keeping good records and mistakes are minimal. Right? How do you know that for sure?

In reality, just because a bookkeeper is an 'expert' and probably knows more than you do about the bookkeeping for your business, it doesn't necessarily mean that what they are doing is right.

Taking an active interest in all aspects of the financial health and wellness of your business is just imperative when you are a small business owner. While it's easy to take a back seat in this department and just let the bookkeeper do their thing, it's not a good business decision to do so.

You owe it to yourself and your business, and to that book-keeper as well to have a hand in things just to make sure that your business doesn't end up in a financial predicament, and also to protect the business from potential fraud that could be conducted by a bookkeeper that just can't help themselves. We've all heard stories about the long-standing employees that embezzled thousands from their employers over the course of so many years. Don't let that be you!

As your business continues to grows, you should implement certain 'checks' that are done during the monthly book-keeping cycle. These checks will allow the burden of processes to not be placed on one person. Some checks you can insert into your process are:

- One person should complete the reconciliation of the bills and statements. They should also enter them into the system.
- Then another person double checks the details of what was done, as well as sets up payments at the bank.
- A third person (business owner, you!) can approve the payments.
- One person can be in charge of the petty cash system; receiving info for the petty cash system as well as issuing cash as it is requested through the petty cash system.

Then another person can reconcile the cash boxes at month end.

Some of the most common tasks completed during book-keeping and record keeping include:

- Enter transactions in your cash ledger and apply them to the correct accounts with the correct sales tax options
- Process bank reconciliations for the main account, savings accounts
- Prepare sales invoices
- Enter purchase invoices
- Prepare a creditors report and upload batch payments to the bank
- Keep in contact with overdue debtors
- Prepare a sales report
- Process payroll and set up payments to employees
- Process payroll tax reports to the tax department and set up payment
- Process sales tax returns and set up payment to the tax department
- Prepare the monthly reports
- Advise you on the actual state of your business finances and give you ideas on how to improve cash flow.

The number one most important report for any business, even a sole-proprietor or self-employed individual, is a profit and loss statement. You need to be able to see your income, minus your expenses in order to see your business's health. Are you running at a profit or a loss? Are you spending more than you're earning? Do you have too many expenses?

The profit and loss statement is one business report that can be run from bookkeeping records for any period of time you choose. Run one for the month, the year, maybe quarterly? Any of these time periods can be helpful glimpses.

This report is also a good one to use when you are trying to calculate how much you should pay the government in taxes.

Remember that a profit and loss report, just like any other report, is only as good as the data that is in your book-keeping system. Keeping accurate and complete records that are up to date is the most essential function when it comes to bookkeeping. If you don't do so, your profit and loss state-ment is no good to you.

The profit and loss statement should list your business income and expenses. It is also sometimes referred to as an Income and Expense report, a Statement of Financial Perfor-mance, or an Income Statement.

A good profit and loss statement will include the following information:

- All of the income for your business
- All of the costs of goods sold by your business
- All of the business's expenses that are deductible
- The accounting statement of profit or loss result

A profit and loss statement does not need to include the information that is listed on a Balance Sheet, which is:

- Business Assets
- Business Liabilities
- Business Equity

How Often Should A Profit And Loss Report Be Produced

Your profit and loss statement can be produced as often as you need to see it. You can pull one daily, weekly, monthly, quarterly, and annually. In general, it's a good idea to prepare this report at least once a month so that you can keep an eye on your business's financial wellbeing. Whether you use the accrual-based method or cash basis method of accounting, you can still create a profit and loss statement.

Some uses for the profit and loss statement report are as follows.

Profit And Loss Reports - What Are They Used For?

A profit and loss report is used to calculate tax.

If it is found that a profit has been earned, that amount is used to calculate income tax that is payable by your business to the government. This calculation should be done at the end of every fiscal/financial year (12 month period). This is done at the end of every financial year (every 12 months).

If it is found that the year-end shows a loss of income, then typically there will not be any income tax to pay. Business losses are tax deductible; however, they don't show financial health for the business and likely will affect the day to day running of the business because you likely won't have enough cash flow to cover expenses.

Loan Applications

When a business applies for a financial loan, whatever entity is providing the loan will likely want to see a profit and loss statement for the business. They will use this statement to determine if it is viable for them to loan money to the busines at this point in time. If your business is consistently operating at a loss, this will show and the profit and loss statement and might be a deterrent for the bank to proceed with a loan.

To Check The Cost Of Goods Sold

To help the bookkeeper pin-point if the business is recouping its cost of goods sold. i.e. is the business on-charging to customers all the direct costs it incurred to complete a job?

Analyze Business Trading Trends

Charting monthly summary of figures that are taken from a profit and loss statement for a month can show the business's trading trends, like rise and fall of expenses versus income.

Charting this can give you as the business owner a way to analyze what is happening in your business, and try to figure out why certain changes are present across different months when it comes to profit/loss levels. When you can look at these things, it could be easy to realize why a certain month's profit was much higher than another's, etc.

An Aid To Improving Business Operations

The profit and loss statement also can help you and your managers figure out how to improve the operations within your business in order to cut down on expenses and help raise your profits. It allows you to see a problem and plan ahead for the next month to try and make a change in for the positive.

The Profit And Loss Statement Accuracy

As mentioned above, this report is based on all income and expenses which are earned or spent by a business.

The accuracy of this statement is only as good as the entries that are made into the bookkeeping system by the book-keeper or owner. This is why it is important to:

- Know what type of expenses can be included as deductible expenses (ones that reduce tax payable) - claiming personal expenses as business ones is not acceptable
- Enter all money earned so that the business is not under-declaring income - doing so means you pay less tax but you can be penalized by the tax department if they find out
- Ensure balance sheet type payments go on the balance sheet and not the profit and loss statement - such as loan repayments, personal expenses, asset purchases
- Process a reconciliation for each bank account,

credit card or online payment system like PayPal, at least once a month to ensure that all payment transactions are captured and included in the accounts

6

BUSINESS TAXES

*W*hen you own a business, you need to know about the different types of taxes that you and your business are subject to paying. Which of these taxes you pay and how you have to pay them depends on what type of business entity you run.

THE FIVE MAIN TYPES OF BUSINESS TAX

Let's go over the five general types of taxes that businesses deal with.

INCOME TAX

Unless your business is a partnership, you will be required to file an annual income tax return for your business. If you are a partnership, you file an information return.

When you file an income tax return, there are specific forms you will need to fill out and turn in, depending on what type of business you are running. (You can refer to the table in Chapter 3 to review the types of forms that are filed for each type of business)

Federal income tax is considered pay as you go, meaning you should be paying on it during the entire year. For a business, you will likely be paying estimated tax quarterly during the year. If you are not being required to pay estimated taxes for your business, you should pay whatever taxes are due at the time of filing.

What Is Income Tax?

Income tax may be a sort of tax that governments impose on income generated by businesses and individuals within their jurisdiction. By law, taxpayers must file a tax return annually to work out their tax obligations.

Income taxes are a source of revenue for governments. They are wont to fund public services, pay government obligations, and supply goods for citizens.

Income tax may be a sort of tax that governments impose on income generated by businesses and individuals within their jurisdiction.

Business income taxes apply to corporations, partnerships, small businesses, and other people who are self-employed.

Personal tax may be a sort of income tax that's levied on a person's wages, salaries, and other sorts of income.

Income tax is used to fund public services, pay government obligations, and provide goods for citizens.

How Income Tax Works

Most countries employ a progressive income tax system in which higher-income earners pay a higher tax rate compared to their lower-income counterparts. The U.S. imposed the nation's first tax in 1862 to assist financing needed for the war. After the war, the tax was repealed, but it was reinstated during the early 20th century.

In the United States, the Internal Revenue Service (IRS) collects taxes and enforces tax law. The IRS employs a complex set of rules and regulations regarding reportable and taxable income, deductions, and credits.

They collect taxes on all forms of income, such as wages, salaries, commissions, investments, and business earnings

The personal tax the govt collects can help fund government programs and services, like Social Security, national security, schools, and roads.

Types of Income Tax

Individual Income Taxes

Individual tax is additionally mentioned as personal taxes. This type of tax is levied on a person's wages, salaries, and other sorts of income. This tax is typically a tax the state imposes. Because of exemptions, deductions, and credits, most individuals do not pay taxes on all of their income.

The IRS offers a series of tax deductions and tax credits that taxpayers can make use of to scale back their taxable income. While a deduction can lower your taxable income and therefore the rate that's wont to calculate your tax, a decrease reduces your tax by supplying you with a larger refund of your withholding.

The IRS offers tax deductions for healthcare expenses, investments, and certain education expenses. For example, if a taxpayer earns $100,000 in income and qualifies for $20,000 in deductions, the taxable income reduces to $80,000 ($100,000 - $20,000 = $80,000).12

Tax credits exist to assist reduce the taxpayer's tax obligation or amount owed. They were created primarily for those in middle-income and low-income households. To illustrate, if an individual owes $20,000 in taxes but qualifies for $4,500 in credits, their tax obligation reduces to $15,500 ($20,000 - $4,500 = $15,500).

Business Income Taxes

Businesses also pay income taxes on their earnings; the IRS taxes income from corporations, partnerships, self-employed contractors, as well as small businesses. The way a business it taxed depends on the business structure, either the corporation, its owners, or shareholders report their business income then deduct their operating and capital expenses. Generally, the difference between their business income and their operating and capital expenses is considered their taxable business income.

Estimated Tax

Estimated taxes are paid by sole proprietors, partners, and S corporation shareholders when they are expecting to owe more than $1000 in taxes for the year when their return is filed. They are also paid by C Corporations if they are expecting to owe more than $500 in taxes for the year when their return is filed.

Figuring estimated tax is done by estimating what your expected gross income will be, what your taxable income will be, and what your deductions, credits and taxes will be for the year. You can then use a worksheet provided by the IRS in Form 1040-ES to figure the estimated tax amount.

In general, estimated tax payments should be turned in quarterly, however, if it's easier for your business to pay them more frequently, you can do so.

Anyone who pays too little tax through withholding, income tax payments or a mixture of the 2 may owe a penalty. In some cases, the penalty may apply if their income tax payments are late, albeit they're due a refund.

For tax year 2019, the penalty will generally apply to anyone who pays but 90 percent of the tax reported on their 2019 tax return during the year through withholding, estimated tax payments or a combination of the two. People who base their income tax payments on last year's tax will normally avoid a penalty if they pay one hundred pc of the quantity shown on Line 15 of their 2018 Form 1040 (110 percent if their income was more than $150,000).

Exceptions to the penalty and special rules apply to some groups of taxpayers, like farmers, fishermen, casualty and disaster victims, those that recently became disabled and up to date retirees. In addition, anyone who receives income unevenly during the year can often avoid or lower the penalty by annualizing their income and making unequal payments throughout the year.

The IRS has seen an increasing number of taxpayers subject to income tax penalties, which apply when someone under-pays their taxes. The number of individuals who paid this penalty jumped from 7.2 million in 2010 to 10 million in 2015, a rise of nearly 40 percent. The penalty amount varies, but are often several hundred dollars.

The IRS urges taxpayers to see into their options to avoid these penalties. Adjusting withholding on their paychecks or the quantity of their income tax payments can help prevent penalties. This is especially important for people within the sharing economy, those with quite one job and people with major changes in their life, sort of a recent marriage or a new child.

There are some simple tips to help taxpayers

- Having enough tax withheld or making quarterly income tax payments during the year can assist you avoid problems at tax time.
- Taxes are pay-as-you-go. This means that you simply have to pay most of your tax during the year, as you receive income, instead of paying at the top of the year.

There are two ways to pay tax:

1. Withholding from your pay, your pension or certain government payments, like Social Security.
2. Making quarterly estimated tax payments during the year.

This will assist you avoid a surprise bill once you file your return. You can also avoid interest or the income tax Penalty for paying insufficient tax during the year. Ordinarily, you'll avoid this penalty by paying a minimum of 90 percent of your tax during the year.

Self-Employment Tax

Self-Employment taxes are basically social security and Medicare tax that individuals who work for themselves pay. They are also referred to as SE Tax. SE taxes that you pay ensure your coverage under the social security system. Social security is a system that gives you coverage for disability and retirement benefits, survivor benefits, as well as hospital insurance benefits (aka Medicare).

If you've earned more than $400 in net earnings from your self-employment, you are required to pay self-employment tax.

. . .

Employment Tax

Employment taxes are paid when you have employees in your business. We'll go over these more in Chapter 8, but for now, a basic glance at employment tax that you must apply and pay on behalf of your employees and your business includes:

- Social Security and Medicare Taxes
- Federal Income Withholding
- Federal Unemployment Tax (FUTA)

People who are self-employed have to pay self-employment taxes, which are Social Security and Medicare taxes.

You have to pay self-employment taxes if:

- Your net earnings are $400 or more
- You work for a church or a qualified church-controlled organization that elected an exemption from Social Security and Medicare taxes, and you make $108.28 or more in wages. This does not apply to ministers or members of a religious order such as nuns or monks.

Excise Tax

Excise taxes are something that not every business has to pay. If you do any of the following, excise taxes are something you will have to deal with:

- Receive payments for certain types of services
- Run certain businesses
- Make or sell specific products
- Use various types of products, facilities, or equipment.

Some of the businesses and products etc that are currently involved in excise tax are:

- Gasoline
- Indoor Tanning Services
- Aircraft Management Services
- Sports Wagering
- Coal
- Sport Fishing
- Archery

There are also various excise taxes depending on the type of business. They could be anything from taxes on sales of tobacco and alcohol, to tax from purchasing a heavy-duty vehicle. These types of taxes are commonly referred to as sin taxes.

Married Couples Who Are In Business Together

Employment tax requirements for family employees can vary from those tax requirements that apply to other employees within the business. There are some issues you should consider when you are running a business as a married couple.

Social Security Benefits

A spouse is considered an employee if there is an employer/employee type of relationship, i.e., the first spouse substantially controls the business in terms of management decisions and the second spouse is under the direction and control of the first spouse. If such a relationship exists, then the second spouse is an employee subject to income tax and FICA (Social Security and Medicare) withholding.

If both spouses share the same level of control when it comes to the affairs of the business, provide basically the same level of service to the business, and both contribute capital to the business, then this can be considered a partnership type of business relationship and the business income would be recorded using Form 1065, US Return of Partnership Income.

If Your Spouse Is Your Employee

When your spouse is in fact your employee and not your partner, you are required to pay Social Security and Medicare taxes for him or her. The wages for the services of a private who works for his or her spouse during a trade or business are subject to tax withholding and Social Security and Medicare taxes, but not to FUTA tax.

Election for Married Couples Unincorporated Businesses

For tax years beginning after New Year's Eve in 2006, the Small Business and Work Opportunity Tax Act of 2007 (Public Law 110-28) provides that a "qualified venture," whose only members are a married couple filing a tax return, can elect to not be treated as a partnership for Federal tax purposes.

You're Married... Should You Really Treat Your Business As A Partnership?

When a business is jointly owned and operated by a married couple and is treated as a partnership for tax reasons, the spouses must comply with filing and record keeping requirements imposed on partnerships and their partners. Married co-owners failing to file properly as a partnership may are reporting on a Schedule C within the name of 1 spouse, in order that just one spouse received credit for social security and Medicare coverage purposes. The election permits certain married co-owners to avoid filing partnership returns, as long as each spouse separately reports a share of all of the businesses' items of income, gain, loss, deduction, and credit. Under the election, both spouses will receive credit for Social Security and Medicare coverage purposes.

What Is A Qualified Joint Venture?

A qualified venture may be a venture that conducts a trade or business where:

(1) the sole members of the venture are a marriage who file a joint return,
(2) both spouses materially participate within the trade or business, and
(3) both spouses elect to not be treated as a partnership.

A qualified venture, for purposes of this provision, includes only businesses that are owned and operated by spouses as co-owners, and not within the name of a state law entity (including a limited partnership or indebtedness company).

Just joint ownership of property that is not a trade or business does not qualify for the election as a joint venture. Both spouses have to share the income, gain, loss, deduction, and credit in accordance with each spouse's interest in the business.

Reporting Federal Income Tax as a Qualified Joint Venture (Including Self-Employment Tax)

When spouses elect to be known as qualified joint venture status, they are treated as sole proprietors when it comes to Federal taxation. The spouses must share the businesses' items of income, gain, loss, deduction, and credit. Therefore, the spouses must take under consideration the things in accordance with each spouse's interest within the business.

This same allocation will apply for calculating self-employment tax if applicable, and may affect each spouse's social security benefits. Each spouse must file a separate Schedule C (or Schedule F) to report profits and losses and, if otherwise required, a separate Schedule SE to report self-employment tax for each spouse. Spouses with a rental land business not otherwise subject to self-employment tax must check the QJV box on Line 2 of Schedule E.

If either of the spouses have $400 or more of other net earnings, the spouse(s) with the other net earnings from self-employment should file Schedule SE without including the amount of internet take advantage of the rental land business from Schedule E on line 2. If the election is formed for a farm rental business that's not included in self-employment, file two Forms 4835 rather than Schedule F.

BUSINESS TAX RATES

Okay, we've gone over the various sorts of taxes that companies pay. Let's mention what the rates are. There are two alternative ways your business is often found out which way determines what your rates are going to be.

1. C Corporations

This one is easy-peasy (sort of). The Tax Cuts and Jobs Act of 2018—aka the tax reform bill—cut the tax rate to a flat 21% for all businesses that are found out as C corporations. Simple enough, right? But there's another thing.

If the corporation pays dividends, shareholders pay taxes on those on their personal tax returns. So, C corporation profits are taxed twice.

There are two sorts of dividends: qualified and unqualified. Let's take a glance at those:

Qualified: If you've owned the stock for extended than 60 days, that dividend is qualified. Qualified dividends get favorable tax rates and are taxed at long-term financial gain rates.

Unqualified: Also referred to as ordinary dividends, these are taxed at the shareholder's regular tax rate (more thereon below!).

2. Pass-Through Entities

The rate for pass-through entities is that the same because the owner's income rate. There's also an alternate minimum tax (AMT). The AMT only applies to certain high-income earners who may otherwise avoid paying a person income taxes.

For review, the kinds of companies that are considered pass-through entities are:

Sole Proprietorship

A business where you're the sole owner. you're the boss and totally liable for everything that happens. It's really important to stay your personal finances and business finances separate so you don't get into any tax trouble.

Partnership (Limited and Limited Liability)

A business owned by two or more people. Limited partnerships (LPs) have a greater potential for private conflict between the partners, since just one of the partners has unlimited liability— this means they're on the hook for any debts or bills if the business goes bad.

The partners with indebtedness also tend to possess limited control of the business. during a indebtedness partnership (LLP), however, all partners are shielded from debts and obligations against the partnership.

Limited Liability Company (LLC)

LLCs help separate personal assets and liabilities from business ones, reducing your personal risk if your business is unable to pay its bills. In an LLC, your profits and losses can undergo to your income without facing corporate taxes, but members of an LLC are considered self-employed and must pay self-employment taxes.

S Corporation

An S corporation is structured to avoid the double taxation that happens during a C corporation. S corporations allow profits, and a few losses, to pass directly through to the owners' income without being subject to corporate tax rates. But there are some limits to S corporations: You can't have quite 100 shareholders, and every one shareholders must be U.S. citizens. Plus, S corporations still need to follow strict filing and operational processes.

State and Native Taxes on Businesses

Depending on where you live, you'll even have to pay state and native taxes. The kinds and amounts of taxes you'll pay are different counting on your location. This is often where a tax pro can really be available and come in handy. Our small-business tax Endorsed Local Providers (ELPs) specialize in the local. They should live in your community so that they may guide you through the complex state, county or city tax laws.

You should also be aware of a few types of state and local taxes too. These are:

State income taxes

Not all states charge income taxes, but the vast majority do, so unless you are one of the lucky ones who lives in a state that is tax free, your business will be required to pay state income taxes.

Property taxes

If you own commercial property, you will have to pay property taxes, which are typically assessed at the county or city level.

Sales taxes

If your business sells things, your business is responsible for collecting sales taxes when applicable. If your business sells things online, the lines get a little fuzzy. This is because some states require that you charge based on where you, the seller, are located. Other states do just the opposite, requiring that you charge taxes based on rates for the state in which your buyer is located. Fun right?

Find Someone That Can Help You With Your Business Taxes

As a business owner, you are well aware by now that business taxes are a pain in the rear. In fact, they are a such a hassle that most small business owners spend a crazy number of hours each tax year on keeping up the books and keeping things straight for taxes.

We don't have to tell you that is time you could have been spending on furthering your business, getting to know and spending time with your customers and serving their needs, tending to your employee's training, or pretty much anything else related to your business that you could have been doing other than those fabulous taxes.

This is yet another reason why it's important to find someone that can help you with your business taxes. You can tell by now this is a point we are really trying to drive home. It will pay off in the long run to have the help of a tax professional and/or accountant.

7

TAX DEDUCTIONS

*Y*ou probably hear about this subject every year at tax time, even if you have only ever filed individual tax returns before now. But most likely you started to hear about them more when you started your small business. Tax deductions. You can deduct this, you can deduct that, that's a deduction save that receipt!

A tax deduction is a certain expense that you incur during your tax year that the government will allow you to take away from your taxable income, thus, saving you money by making your taxable income lower. They are available for both businesses and individuals.

There are literally hundreds of deductions available for use when it comes to figuring your tax return, but most people don't know about them or what they are. This is when a tax professional or accountant comes in handy. It's their job to know about all of these deductions and how to apply them to you and your business if they can.

Using a tax professional or accountant to do your tax return could be a choice that saves you thousands of dollars that you weren't even aware you could claim. But don't wait to hire them until the end of your tax year. Meet with a tax professional or accountant at the beginning of the year so that they can guide you in regards to what deductions might come into play for you during the year. If you're able to know what is available, you can plan ahead accordingly during the tax year and take advantage of deductions that can be useful for your business.

Deductions are not just for big corporations or multi-million-dollar companies. They are there for use on any level as an individual or business, so go find out what is out there for you!

Let's talk about some of the common deductions and what they are.

ABOVE THE LINE DEDUCTIONS

An above the line deduction is a deduction to your gross income. When completing tax returns, you take the total of the above the line deductions away from your gross income amount to get what is known as your adjusted gross income (AGI). Anyone who files using a Form 1040 can claim above the line deductions.

STANDARD OR ITEMIZED DEDUCTIONS?

It's recommended that if your itemized deductions, or deductions that you take throughout the year like purchases that qualify, etc, are smaller than the standard deduction, you obviously want to claim the standard deduction. But if your itemized deductions are greater than the current standard deduction, you will want to itemize.

STANDARD DEDUCTIONS

A standard deduction is a flat amount that the IRS provides and allows you to subtract from your adjusted gross income amount, based on what your filing status is. Standard deductions are only used when you don't itemize your deductions.

The standard deduction amounts for the 2019 tax year were:

- Head of Household - $18,350
- Married filing jointly - $24,400
- Single, or married filing separately - $12,200

ITEMIZED DEDUCTIONS

Itemized deductions are also amounts that are subtracted from your adjusted gross income. Itemized deductions are things that you paid for throughout the year that qualify for a particular deduction. There is no limit on the number of itemized deductions you can take.

Some examples of itemized deductions that you can claim with your taxes are:

Gambling Losses

Obviously, your business is likely not going to have any gambling losses, but on your individual return, you can deduct this. You can write off losses, but the amount you write off can't be greater than what you report for your gambling income. So, if you won $5,000 during the tax year but you also lost $7,000, you could write off $5,000 in losses because you can't claim more in losses than what you won. Also remember that you can't report losses without reporting your winnings as well. And you need to make sure you've got a log of where, when, and how much you gambled to include with your return.

Personal Property Tax

There are deductions available for taxes on personal property such as cars or boats.

Local and State Income or Sales Tax Paid

Deduction of up to $10,000 ($5,000 if your filing status is married filing separately) for state and local sales, property and income taxes.

Self-Owned Business

When you own your own business, you can deduct sales tax on business purchases, office equipment, your health insurance premiums, and anything else that is deemed a regular and necessary cost in order to perform your business.

Charity

If you donated to a charitable organization, you can look at the IRS's Tax-Exempt Organization page on their website in order to search for the organization to see if they are eligible to be claimed as a tax-deductible donation.

Real Estate Taxes and Points

The definition of a point is 1% of a home loan's value. When you get a home loan, banks charge you a fee, and this fee is shown in points. You can write off these points when you do your taxes.

* * *

Mortgage Interest for your Home

Most of the time, you are able to deduct the whole figure in interest that you paid to your mortgage company in the current tax year.

Student Loan Interest

You can claim up to $2500 of interest paid towards student loans during the current tax year. Even if your parents paid this interest, you can still deduct it on your own tax return as long as your parents don't claim you as a dependent.

Expenses That Are Job Related That Aren't Reimbursed By Your Employer

These expenses can be union dues, uniforms that your job requires that you purchase and wear to work, as well as gas and repairs for your vehicle if it is used for business-related reasons.

Rent

If you have a business that rents any kind of property or equipment, you are able to deduct the cost of rent for that property or equipment. You cannot own even partially the property or equipment in question. Another deduction when it comes to rent and rental agreements is that if you for some reason have to end a business lease, the cost to do so is deductible as well.

Home Office

This one can be a bit tricky. If you are working from home, or if you use a part of your home in your business, self-employment tax deductions are available to you, but you have to be careful how you calculate them. Here is some more info:

There are a couple of ways to do this. The simple way's method allows you to deduct $5/sq foot of home that you use for your business, but only up to 300 square feet. Still, that's a pretty good-sized space, measuring roughly 17 feet by 17 feet. You don't need to keep as many records this way, but the deduction amount might end up smaller than the other method, so calculate both ways before deciding which is best.

The more complicated way to deduct this is to figure up the percentage of your house's square footage that you have dedicated to your business. Then whatever that percentage is, is the percentage of your costs that are deductible. So, for example, if your home office eats up around 15% of your home's square footage, then 15% of your housing costs (mortgage, rent, property taxes, maintenance and repairs, utilities, etc) might be eligible for deduction. You'll want to refer to the IRS Publication 587 for more detailed info, or, of course, ask your tax professional or accountant about this deduction and how it could possibly apply to your situation.

Continuing Education

When you run a business, there is no limit on the number of things you have to learn that can help grow the business. Believe it or not, there are self-employment tax deductions for your continuing education expenses.

You can deduct the cost of "qualifying work-related education". The deduction requires that the education you are taking part in has to "maintain or improve skills needed in your present work". This deduction includes supplies, lab fees, books and tuition, and even includes transportation costs to get to and from classes.

Your Car

Whether it's driving to meet your vendors, making pickups and wooing clients can be hard on your car. There are a few self-employment tax deductions that might help you recover some dollars for that wear and tear.

You can deduct a little more than $1 per every two miles you have put on your car for those business purposes.

At the end of the tax year, figure up the number of miles you drove in your own car for business reasons, then multiply that by the IRS' standard mileage rate which is currently 57.5 cents per mile in 2020. Then, deduct the total you come up with. Make sure to keep a mileage log; you'll need to provide it if you're audited.

You can choose to deduct your "actual car expenses" instead. These actual expenses include depreciation, licenses, gas, oil, tolls, parking fees, garage rent, lease payments, insurance, registration fees, repairs and your tires. You might have to do it this way if you're using more than four cars in your business. If you're leasing your car, read IRS Publication 463 for their rules about the amount of lease payments you can deduct on your taxes.

Self-Employment Taxes

One really odd deduction, but a great one, is that you can deduct half of your self-employment tax on your federal income taxes. So, if you paid $3,000 during the year towards self-employment tax, you can deduct $1500 of that on your Form 1040 when it comes time to do your taxes.

C Corporations and Limited Liability Companies do not qualify for this tax deduction.

Premiums For Business Insurance

Business insurance, employee health insurance and employee accident premiums are eligible for deduction.

Schedule C on your tax form has an area specifically for this. Make sure to review IRS Publication 535 for details on how to deduct the right type of premium.

In addition to employee health insurance premiums qualifying, if you are self-employed, you may be able to deduct some of your own health insurance premiums as well.

Office Supplies

Every business needs office supplies to get them through day to day running of their business. You can deduct pens, staples, paper, postage, and similar items. In most cases, you deduct the cost of office supplies that you actually used during the tax year. However, if you have office supplies on hand that you don't usually inventory or record the use of, those are typically deductible in the year you buy them, too.

For computers or special equipment that are larger purchases, the general rule is that you can deduct them in the year you buy them if their useful lives are a year or less. If their useful lives are longer than a year, the IRS may view those things as assets that depreciate over time. Even though this means not being able to deduct the full cost of the item all at once, you likely can deduct the depreciation on the item over its useful life.

. . .

Interest On Loans And Credit Cards

Check your credit card statements for potential self-employment tax deductions. Interest accrued on purchases that were business expenses. You can't deduct credit card interest accrued from business expenses if the purchase was made on someone else's credit card, for instance. You don't necessarily need to have a business card to deduct qualifying interest charges. If you use a personal card exclusively for business expenses, for example, you can generally still deduct the interest charges.

Internet And Phone Costs

Anyone from real estate agents and journalists to day care providers and jewelry makers could deduct part or all of their annual cell phone or internet bill. You can deduct your entire bill if you have a dedicated business cell phone or internet connection. You must use your smartphone or internet service for business, and your employer — if you have one — must not reimburse you. If you don't have a dedicated line, you can deduct the percentage used for business.

Business Meals and Business Travel

Whether it's for a flight across the country or an overnight on the other side of the state, expenses for travel and food can be self-employment tax deductions. Flights, hotels, taxis and food are deductible business expenses as long as they're for actual, legitimate business purposes. You can't deduct travel expenses for your spouse, your kids, or other people unless that person is your employee. Generally, you can deduct 50% of the cost of a meal if the meal was business-related, was not "lavish or extravagant," you or your employee were at the meal, one of your business contacts got the meal, and the cost of the meal didn't include a charge for entertainment.

Instead of deducting the actual cost of each meal, which can require a lot of receipt hoarding, you can use a standard daily meal allowance. Under this method, you deduct a flat amount instead of recording every single meal expense (consider keeping your receipts anyway so that you can prove your deduction if you're audited).

Start-Up Costs

You might be able to deduct start-up costs from starting your own business. Start-up costs generally refer to what it costs to set up the business and get it ready before actually opening. Some of these costs might be advertising, consulting fees, travel to work out suppliers and to gain customers, and wages for employee training.

It might be possible to deduct up to $5,000 of your start-up costs as well as $5,000 of your organizational costs (whatever it cost you to set up the legal entity of your business, i.e. LLC).

Not everyone will be able to use this deduction. If your start-up or organizational costs exceed $50,000, your deduction is reduced by however much your cost went over that amount.

Many brand-new startups make the error of thinking initial business expenses aren't deductible until their businesses are fully operational. However, the IRS allows small business owners to deduct a good array of startup expenses before beginning business operations.

The IRS allows you to deduct up to $5,000 in business startup costs and up to $5,000 in organizational costs, but only if your total startup costs are $50,000 or less. With the assistance of your tax software or a tax expert, you'll write off typical costs related to fixing a business during tax filing.

Typical costs to line up a business include business insurance, office space, land, office supplies, business cards, business assets, professional fees (i.e. hiring accountants), and small business loan fees. If you're operating your business from a headquarters, you'll qualify for a headquarters deduction.

Additional costs also can include employee training, locating suppliers, and advertising to potential clients. While companies cannot deduct licensing and incorporation fees as startup expenses, these costs could also be deductible as organizational expenses.

It's important to recollect that startup founders can only deduct those expenses resulting in the creation of a viable business entity. If you opt against forming your business, the above costs are going to be labeled as personal expenses, and you'll not be ready to deduct any of your costs.

Advertising for Your Business

Advertising expenses that are directly related to your business can be deductible. You can usually deduct advertising "to keep your name before the public if it relates to business you reasonably expect to gain in the future," which gives the green light to advertising encouraging people to take part in a particular cause, such as donating blood.

The type of advertising matters. Generally, you can't deduct lobbying expenses. Also, you can't deduct advertising in a convention program of a political party, or in any other publication if any of the proceeds from the publication are for, or intended for, the use of a political party or candidate. There's a line on Schedule C dedicated to reporting your advertising expenses.

Subscriptions To Publications

The amount that you spend on magazines, books, and journals, in the niche that is directly related to your type of business is tax deductible.

For example, if you run a wedding dress shop, and you have a monthly subscription to "Modern Bride" magazine, that subscription would be tax deductible because it directly relates to the type of business that you do. However, if you had a monthly subscription to "Sports Illustrated" magazine, that would not be deductible because it is not closely related to your line of business.

Select Membership Fees

If you belong to a professional organization, you may be able to deduct the membership fee. You can't count memberships in clubs (especially country clubs and travel-related clubs). However, the IRS carves out exceptions for memberships to boards of trade, business leagues, chambers of commerce, civic or public service organizations, professional organizations such as bar associations and medical associations, real estate boards and trade associations.

For the IRS, a big indication that a membership isn't deductible is whether one of the organization's main purposes is to provide you or your guests with entertainment or access to entertainment facilities.

Qualified Business Income Deduction

The qualified business income deduction (QBI) allows eligible self-employed and small-business owners to deduct a portion of their business income on their taxes. If your total taxable income — that's, not just your business income but other income also — is at or below $163,300 for single filers or $326,600 for joint filers, then in 2020 you'll qualify for the 20% deduction on your taxable business income.

The qualified business income deduction is for people that have "pass-through income" — that's business income that you simply report on your personal income tax return. Entities eligible for the qualified business income deduction include sole proprietorship s, partnerships, S corporations and limited liability companies (LLCs).

Pass-through income

This deduction may be a product of the Tax Cuts and Jobs Act and is meant to assist small-business owners economize. U.S. taxpayers can now use the maximum amount as 20% of their pass-through income as a deduction. This includes income from an LLC, S-Corporation, or sole proprietorship, also as partnership income and income from rental land, just to call a number of the potential sources. The deduction isn't available to certain taxpayers whose income comes from "specified service businesses" and exceeds certain thresholds.

TAX CREDITS

Tax credits are defined as a dollar-for-dollar reduction to the amount of your actual tax bill. Some credits are considered refundable, but not many. What this means is that if you owe $400 in taxes, but you qualify for a tax credit in the amount of $1200, you will get a check for the difference of $800.

Tax credits can reduce your tax bill more than deductions can because they are truly a dollar for dollar amount taken off of your bill.

A tax credit is a form of tax incentive that is designed to encourage a certain activity, or to ease the financial burden on American families associated with certain situations. For example, the Child Tax Credit is intended to help cover the high costs of raising a child in the United States, while the Lifetime Learning Credit is designed to encourage Americans to pursue educational opportunities.

Unlike a tax deduction, which reduces your taxable income, a tax credit reduces your tax liability dollar-for-dollar. If you calculate your taxable income and apply the 2020 tax brackets, and find that you simply owe the IRS $5,000, a $1,000 decrease would scale back your liabilities to $4,000.

The Most Common Tax Credits Available In The United States

There is a long list of tax credits Americans could potentially qualify for, but many are very specialized and uncommon. On the other hand, there are some tax credits that millions of Americans qualify for, and here are eight of them:

- Child Tax Credit
- Credit for other dependents
- Child and Dependent Care Credit
- Earned Income Tax Credit (EITC)
- The Retirement Contribution Savings Credit (Saver's Credit)
- American Opportunity Tax Credit (AOTC)
- Lifetime Learning Credit (LLC)
- Earned Income Credit

An earned income credit is a tax credit that is figured and limited by the number of dependent children, income level, and your filing status.

Earned Income Tax Credit

One of the most substantial credits for taxpayers is the Earned Income Tax Credit. Established in 1975—in part to offset the burden of Social Security taxes and to provide an incentive to work—the EITC is determined by income and is phased in according to filing status: single, married filing jointly or either of those with children. Eligibility and therefore the amount of the credit are supported adjusted gross income, earned income and investment income.

- A person must be a minimum of 25 years old and younger than 65 to qualify.
- If married, both spouses must have valid Social Security numbers and must have lived in the country for more than six months.
- If you'll be claimed as a hooked in to another filer's income tax return, you are not going to qualify.

Reasons That You Will Not Qualify For Earned Income Tax Credit:

- If you are married filing separately, and you earned $3,650 or more in 2020 from investment income, that is considered "disqualified income" and you cannot qualify for the credit.
- If you're self-employed, you may still qualify for the Earned Income Tax Credit (EITC). Tax experts recommend you check your eligibility per annum, albeit you think that you will not qualify.

Other self-employed deductions:

Finally, if you're self-employed, there are plenty of business deductions you'll be ready to cash in on. You can deduct business-related travel expenses, office supplies and equipment, and insurance premiums from your self-employment income, just to call a couple of potential deductions. And don't ditch the special retirement accounts for the self-employed that we covered earlier.

Remember that business tax deductions are mostly way more complicated than the simple blurbs in this chapter that we use to describe them. It's tax code. That means it's never simple. But at least now you have a good idea of basic deductions that are out there and available to small business owners like you.

8

PAYROLL TAXES

*I*f your business has employees, you will need to know how to deal with Payroll Taxes. When it comes to payroll taxes, you need to have the knowledge that it takes to properly process information, apply the appropriate taxation, etc. You will need to choose to complete these processes yourself, employee someone that will do it for you, use an outside payroll service, or hire an accountant to do it for you.

Here are some basics on what to know if you plan to process your own payroll.

FEDERAL INCOME TAX WITHHOLDING:

Federal Income tax withholding is the tax that is withheld from your employee's pay for federal income taxes owed by them. How much federal income tax should be withheld is figured by the information that your employee recorded on their Form W-4 when hired. An employee has the right to change their Form W-4 information at any time and as often as they want to.

SOCIAL SECURITY AND MEDICARE:

Also known as FICA taxes (Federal Insurance Contributions Act), these taxes are shared between the employer and employee. The employer deducts half of the total due from the employee's wages/salary, and the employer pays the other half due.

ADDITIONAL MEDICARE TAX:

This tax was added in 2013 when the Affordable Care Act was passed. Employers withhold a 0.9% Additional Medicare Tax on their employee's earnings that go above a certain threshold. The employer is not responsible for matching any of this additional tax.

FEDERAL UNEMPLOYMENT TAX (FUTA):

Paid separately from other taxes and not withheld from employee pay.

SELF-EMPLOYMENT TAX:

For self-employed individuals, the self-employment tax is basically Medicare and Social Security for yourself.

HOW TO PROCESS PAYROLL TAX:

As the employer, you will figure the gross pay for your employee whether this is hourly rate at a number of hours worked, or a percentage of a salary. Then, you will use that gross pay amount to base deductions of specific amounts for federal income tax by using the information on the W-4 form that is current for that employee, and deduct a specific amount for the FICA taxes.

As an employer, you are required to make deposits to social security, Medicare and federal income tax on a monthly or semi-weekly basis of your choosing. For Federal Unemployment Tax (FUTA) you need to deposit for the quarter of the year that your tax due is greater than $500.

For state payroll taxes, which vary from state to state, you will need to check with your state's tax agency for the specific information and rules you need to follow in regards to how to collect and remit payroll taxes, and what different kinds of income are taxed.

HOW TO PAY PAYROLL TAXES:

The payroll tax process involves depositing and reporting taxes to the IRS. After the employer has calculated the amounts for federal income tax withholding and FICA taxes, and withheld these amounts from employee paychecks, they must:

- Calculate the amount they, as a business, must pay for FICA taxes, and set aside those amounts
- Make payments to the IRS either monthly or semi-weekly, based on the size of their total employee payroll
- Report on payroll taxes quarterly using Form 941 or through e-file

Reports and deposits are due by specific dates, and if an employer does not remit payroll taxes or sends them in late, the company could be subject to monetary fines.5 These start at 2% of the past-due amount for payments up to five days late. The penalty increases, up to 15% if the company is past 10 days of non-payment, and the IRS has had to send out a payment notice.

* * *

1. **Have all employees complete a W-4.** To get paid, employees need to complete Form W-4 to document their filing status and keep track of personal allowances. The more allowances or dependents workers have, the less payroll taxes are taken out of their paychecks each pay period. For each new employee you hire, you need to file a new hire report. Note that there is a new version of the Form W-4 for 2020, so this is the form you should have new hires fill out starting January 1, 2020.

2. **Find or sign up for Employer Identification Numbers.** Before you do payroll yourself, make sure you have your Employer Identification Number (EIN) ready. An EIN is kind of like an SSN for your business and is used by the IRS to identify a business entity and anyone else who pays employees. If you don't have one, you can apply for an EIN through Square using our free EIN assistant. You may also need to get a state EIN number; check your state's employer resources for more details.

3. **Choose your payroll schedule.** After you register for your Employer Identification Numbers, get insured (don't forget workers' compensation), and display workplace posters, you need to add three important dates to your calendar: employee

pay dates, tax payment due dates, and tax filing deadlines (read more about basic labor laws here).

4. **Calculate and withhold income taxes.**

When it comes time to pay your employees, you need to determine which federal and state taxes to withhold from your employees' pay by using the IRS Withholding Calculator and your state's resource or a reliable paycheck calculator. You must also keep track of both the employee and employer portion of taxes as you go.

5. **Pay taxes.** When it's time to pay taxes, you need to submit your federal, state, and local tax deposits, as applicable (usually on a monthly basis).

6. **File tax forms & employee W-2s.** Finally, be sure to send in your employer federal tax return (usually each quarter) and any state or local returns, as applicable. And last but not least, don't forget about preparing your annual filings and W-2s at the end of the year.

PROCESS PAYROLL USING A PROCESSING SERVICE

1. **Decide on a payroll processing service.**
Most full-service payroll processing systems will

handle payroll taxes, filings, etc and will have software that is web-based where you can complete your portion of the payroll.

2. **Insert Your Employee Data** - When you are using payroll software, the first step will be to add in your employees and their information into the system. Adding information accurately is essential in getting your payroll to process correctly. Typically, the information needed in these types of systems are the employee's name, social security number, address, and their tax withholding information that is on their current W-4.

3. **Track Working Hours** - When you have employees, you need to keep track of their hours worked per the U.S. Department of Labor. This information needs to be retained for at least 2 years. Some states require that you keep this documentation longer so make sure you check your own state's rules in regards to this as well. If you have payroll software that allows employees to clock in/out, this is sufficient and will act as a 'timecard' that gets approved and sent in for processing.

4. **Process The Payroll** - There will be a send or submit section that will send the information in for processing to the service.

5. **Keep Record Of Your Tax Filings And Tax Payments** - Tax forms are required to be kept for at least 3 years according to the Internal Revenue Service. For state tax filings and payments, the length of time tax forms should be kept varies from state to state, so check with your state tax agency for their specific timeline regarding this.

PROCESS PAYROLL USING AN ACCOUNTANT

If you aren't keen on doing your payroll yourself, or setting up a payroll processing service, your other option is to hire a payroll accountant. A professional accountant will be able to process your payroll while keeping great attention on the details of taxation for your employees, tax payments, and getting filings in and accounted for in a timely manner.

9

LOWER TAX STRATEGIES

When you own a business, it's important to know all about the deductions that are available to you and how to use these strategies to lower your taxes.

There are several write-offs available for small businesses that are commonly used. Let's go over them.

MEALS AND ENTERTAINMENT

This deduction is one you can use, but shouldn't be abused. First off, entertaining clients for business used to be tax deductible, but as of 2018, it is not. Remember this before you book some sort of golf session or another type of entertainment for your clients. The cost solely sits with you. Any recreation or activity that is directly for employees, customers or clients is considered entertainment.

Now, on to meals. You can't deduct the full cost of meals; however, you can deduct 50% of those costs. It may not seem like it's worth it, but it definitely can add up over the course of a full year. Keep those receipts and follow these rules when considering using this deduction.:

- Don't go overboard - Don't abuse the fact that you can write something off and order ten of the most expensive things on the menu. Make sense?
- Make sure the expense is for something that is commonly accepted in your field of business - What we mean by this is, if you own a business that markets itself as a top supporter of local small businesses, you probably don't want to turn in a bunch of receipts for lunches at big chain restaurants. Walk your talk.
- The reason for the expense should be business related and an attempt to bring in revenue - This doesn't mean that the only time you can deduct is when you took those big important clients out for dinner. You can deduct lunches between yourself and your business partner as well if the purpose was to discuss the business.

TRAVEL EXPENSES

Yes, you see that right. When you travel for business, there are deductions at your fingertips. Sometimes as a small business owner, it's tough to find time to take a vacation, am I right? You're so busy the only time you can seem to get away is on a business trip and how fun is that? Well, turns out, it can be.

Have you ever considered making your vacation align with your next business trip? Your trip has to primarily be for business, but why not bring your spouse along and have a little fun while you're there. When you do this, you have your business deductions at your fingertips that can offset the cost of what would have been a whole separate vacation.

First off, remember that days you are doing business are the only days you can actually deduct your expenses, and they have to be your expenses only. Your spouse's expenses are not eligible for deduction unless they too are an employee and it was necessary for them to come on this business trip as well.

What Can I Deduct?

You can deduct the following things on your trip:

- *Food* - Half of your food costs. Remember only your own food costs are eligible here and don't go overboard.
- *Transportation* - The entire amount of your transportation is deductible.
- *Lodging* - The cost of your hotel stay is also completely eligible for deduction.
- *Mobile Office related fees* - These fees are deductible at 100% as well.
- *Laundry* - If you have laundry costs during your stay, you can deduct all of this expense as well.

How Can I Deduct?

There are two different ways you can deduct your eligible travel expenses.

- *Actual Expense Method* - This method really is what it says. Keep all of your receipts for every expense you've had on your trip. It's advisable to have a special place to keep all of your receipts, like a specific zipper pouch or small box. Heck even a Ziploc bag works, just so long as you know where they all are.

Make sure you are also documenting what business you are doing each day and with whom. You have to be able to show that you are there and working for your business on each day you have a business-related expense that you claim.

- ***Per Diem Method*** - You can check the IRS website to find out what the going per diem (per day) rate is for business related expenses allowed when you travel. If you use this method of deduction, even if your expenses were less than the per diem rate for any given day you are doing business on your trip, you can still claim the whole per diem deduction for that day.

One thing to keep in mind is that if you operate a sole-proprietorship, you cannot use the per diem method of deduction for your business trips for lodging, but any of the other expenses are okay.

Tips to Consider

Consider planning ahead as to whether you are going to use the per diem or actual expense method before you travel. If you do so, you can take into consideration what things you might want to skimp on and what things to not.

Just because you have business during a day, it doesn't mean you have to spend the entire day doing business, however, your main purpose for your trip should be business related. That being said, you can vacation it up at your leisure during the hours you don't have business planned.

Remember to not go overboard with your expenses. There is no need to book the presidential suite, or to eat at the most expensive restaurant every night you are in town, etc. Your travel expenses should be regular necessary expenses associated with the travel for your business needs.

You have nothing to worry about as long as you're being fair and are running a legit business.

HOW TO DEDUCT YOUR VEHICLE ON TAXES

Aside from homes or other properties, cars are one of the most expensive things you can own as an individual or a business. They require upkeep, maintenance, gas, and repairs throughout the time you own them.

Did you know that the Internal Revenue Service actually allows some car expenses to be written off if they are used for qualified business reasons? Here are some tax deductions to remember and take advantage of when they apply to vehicles you use in your business.

. . .

Business Use

Business use deductions are especially important for a sole-proprietorship, because you can deduct the cost of using a vehicle for business purposes, even if it is your own personal vehicle.

You'll need to make sure you can document the business use versus the personal use when using this deduction.

Fleet Deductions

Small businesses that own a vehicle or vehicles that are used only for their business can add that vehicle to their tax deductions as part of the operating expenses for the business. Repairs are what you can deduct so when your business vehicle or vehicles have to head to the shop, keep receipts and documentation so that come tax time, you can take advantage of this deduction.

Donate Your Heap To Charity

Maybe you have a vehicle that is on it's last leg and it's no longer cost effective to keep repairing it over and over again. You can donate the car to a charity instead of trying to make a tiny bit of cash off of selling it. Most charities will come and pick the car up from you as well. Remember to get a receipt for your donation so that you can include it in your tax documents. The receipt should show the market value of the vehicle at the time of donation because that is the amount that you will be allowed to deduct.

Previous Hybrid Purchase or Electric Conversions?

Hybrid cars that were purchased before January 1, 2011 can be claimed on your taxes. This unfortunately was a program that was phased out which is why there is a deadline noted. But not everyone knew about this, which is why it is worth mentioning. If you have one that you purchased before that deadline and haven't claimed it yet, do so!

The other program that ended December 31, 2011 was the electric conversion. If you converted your car to electric before that deadline, the tax credit that you can claim is up to $4,000, so again, worth mentioning. If you did this before the deadline and haven't claimed it yet, do it!

Business Expenses In Your Personal Vehicle

If you work for a business and are not being reimbursed for your expenses while using for business purposes, you can deduct these costs on your taxes. The expenses that are allowed are maintenance and fuel cost. You can calculate these by using mileage. The IRS updates the amounts you can deduct using this calculation on a regular basis. Again, make sure that you are keeping a clear record of the business use for the vehicle so that when it comes time to produce documentation, you are ready to go.

OTHER DEDUCTIBLE ITEMS FOR YOUR BUSINESS

If you have employees, there are a couple of other categories of deductions that you could take advantage of.

- ***Company Parties*** - If you hold a party or any other type of social gathering for your company and all employees are invited, you can deduct 100% of the cost. That's right!
- ***Snacks and Meals for the Office*** - Whenever you purchase meals or snacks for your entire company, you can claim 50% of your expense as a deduction.

As with anything in business, don't be extravagant in your use of these deductions. Be honest and fair and make sure you have your documentation, and you will go far with logging in some great tax lowering expenses when it comes time to file.

10

TAX REFORMS

One thing about taxes and tax law and code is that things are ever changing. Tax reform happens all the time. That's why it's important to keep up on current legislation. Just because you think you know all there is to know about your business taxes this year, Congress could pass new bills or laws that change things up.

You can always go to the IRS.gov site to learn about what is currently happening in regards to tax reform. Accountants and tax professionals will be keeping an eye on these things as well so if you hire a professional, they should be able to tell you about upcoming changes you need to know about.

The biggest tax reform bill that has passed in current history was the Tax Cuts and Jobs Act (TCJA) that was approved by

Congress and passed in December of 2017. The TCJA affects both businesses and individuals' taxes.

Let's go over some of the major changes in the bill.

TAX CUTS AND JOBS ACT (TCJA)

In order to best understand how the TCJA affects your small business, seek the advice of a tax professional or accountant.

One of the major changes with the TCJA was the modifications to the tax rates and tax brackets.

For tax years beginning in 2018 through 2025, the Tax Cuts and Jobs Act (TCJA) applies seven altered tax brackets to individuals supported filing status: 10%, 12%, 22%, 24%, 32%, 35%, and 37%. The top rate applies to taxable income over $600,000 for married individuals filing joint returns, or $500,000 for single individuals and heads of households. The TCJA also reduces the tax brackets for estates and trusts to four: 10%, 24%, 35%, and 37%.

The tax bill made changes to deductions, expensing, credits, depreciation, fringe benefits, and other things that could affect your business's tax liability. When reading about tax reform in general, remember to think about the way your business is structured, and what accounting methods you use in order to properly apply new tax reform to your business's own situation.

Standard Deduction Increased

For tax years beginning in 2018 through 2025, the standard deduction is increased to $24,000 for married individuals filing a joint return, $18,000 for head-of-household filers, and $12,000 for all other taxpayers. Inflation applies in tax years beginning after 2018. The current additional standard deduction for the elderly and blind is unchanged.

2017 2018

$6,350/$12,700

$12,000/$24,000

Personal Exemptions Suspended

Previously, taxpayers were allowed a private exemption for themselves, their spouses, and any dependents. The TCJA effectively suspends the deduction for private exemptions by reducing it to zero. This provision sunsets in 2026.

2017 2018

$4,050 for each household member

Suspended

"Kiddie Tax" Modified

Beginning in 2018, the rates for single individuals apply to the portion of a child's taxable income attributable to earned income. A child's taxable net unearned income is taxed at the trust and estate rates (see section above and the enclosed charts). The Kiddie Tax applies to a toddler if he or she is under age 19 at the top of the tax year or may be a full-time student under age 24, with at least one living parent AND his or her unearned income exceeds $2,100.

> ### *2017 2018*
>
> *Child's net unearned income taxed at parent's rate if parent's rate higher than child's*
>
> *Child's earned income taxed at single individual rate*
>
> *Child's net unearned income taxed per trust/estate brackets*
>
> *Child's earned income taxed at single individual rate*

Capital Gains Thresholds Indexed

The TCJA maintains current maximum rates on net capital gains and qualified dividends (0%, 15% and 20%), but indexes the bracket thresholds for inflation in tax years beginning after 2017. For 2018, the 15% breakpoint is $77,200 for joint returns; $51,700 for heads of household; $2,600 for trusts and estates; and $38,600 for other unmarried individuals. The 20% breakpoint is $479,000 for joint returns; $452,400 for heads of household; $12,700 for estates and trusts; and $425,800 for other unmarried individuals.

New Deduction for Pass-Through Income

Previously, income from a pass-through entity (sole proprietorships, partnerships, LLCs, and S corporations) was subject to the rate of the entity's owners or shareholders and reported on their individual returns. For tax years beginning after New Year's Eve , 2017 and before January 1, 2026, the TCJA adds a replacement deduction for taxpayers with qualified business income (QBI) from a pass-through entity. QBI is that the net amount of "qualified items of income, gain, deduction, and loss" concerning any qualified trade or business of the taxpayer. An individual taxpayer generally may deduct 20% of QBI.

The deduction cannot exceed the greater of:

> 50% of the W-2 wages with reference to the qualified trade or business ("W-2 wage limit"), or
> the sum of 25% of the W-2 wages paid with reference to the qualified trade or business plus 2.5% of the unadjusted basis, immediately after acquisition,

of all "qualified property" (tangible, depreciable property used and still available to be used at the top of a given tax year).

The deduction does not apply to the trade or business of being an employee, nor to certain service businesses, such as those offering investment-type activities. However, the service-business exclusion does not apply to taxpayers whose income does not exceed $315,000 married filing jointly or $157,500 for other individuals. The limitation is phased in for those taxpayers over the next $100,000 of income for married filing jointly taxpayers and $50,000 for others.

2017 2018

Subject to owner's income tax rate

20% deduction for domestic business profits, limited to greater of (1) 50% of W-2 wages or (2) 25% of W-2 wages plus 2.5% of the unadjusted basis of qualified property after wage limitation phase-in

Specified service businesses generally not eligible, except for taxpayers with taxable income $157.5k/315k (over the next $50k/$100k)

Special rules apply to certain income from
PTPs and dividends from REITs
Trusts and estates are eligible for the
deduction

Child Tax Credit Increased

For tax years beginning after New Year's Eve, 2017 and before January 1, 2026, the child tax credit is increased to $2,000 for each child under the age of 17, and $500 for certain non-child dependents. The credit is phased out for adjusted gross incomes over $200,000 single or $400,000 married filing joint, and it is refundable via the Additional Child Tax Credit up to $1,400 per child if the credit allowed exceeds the tax owed.

> ### *2017 2018*
> *$1,000 credit per child under age 17*
> *Phased out for AGI > $75,000/ $110,000*
> *Refundable if credit exceeds tax owed via*
> *   additional child tax credit*
> *$2,000 credit per child under age 17 and*
> * $500 per non-child dependent*
> *Phased out for AGI > $200,000 / $400,000*
> *Refundable up to $1,400 per child*

State & Local Tax Deduction Limited

Previously, state or local tax and property taxes paid by a private were fully deductible. For tax years beginning after New Year's Eve, 2017 and before January 1, 2026, full deduction is suspended apart from such taxes or paid in carrying on a trade or business. Partial deduction is permitted up to $10,000 of the aggregate amount of such taxes.

Prepayments of 2018 state or local income tax, made in 2017, will be treated as paid in 2018.

> ### *2017 2018*
>
> *Fully deductible*
>
> *Up to $10,000 of aggregate state/local and*
> *property taxes deductible*
>
> *2017 prepayments of 2018 state/local tax*
> *treated as paid in 2018*

Mortgage Interest Deduction Limited

For tax years beginning after December 31, 2017 and before January 1, 2026, the deduction for interest on home equity loans is suspended. The deduction for mortgage interest on a primary or secondary residence is limited to interest on the first $750,000 of debt. The lower limits don't apply to home loans taken out before December 15, 2017, or to such existing loans that are later refinanced. In tax years beginning after 2025, the previous limitations of $1 million mortgage debt and $100,000 home equity debt are restored, and taxpayers may deduct interest on such loans regardless of when they were taken out.

> ### *2017 2018*
> *Interest deductible on first $1M of mortgage on primary or secondary residence, and first $100k of home equity debt*
> *Interest deductible on first $750,000 of mortgage on primary or secondary residence*
> *No home equity debt deduction*
> *Existing mortgages grandfathered*

Charitable Contribution Deduction Increased

For taxpayers who still itemize deductions after 2017, the 50% limitation for cash contributions to public charities and certain private foundations is increased to 60%. Contributions greater than 60% of a taxpayer's "contribution base" may be carried forward and deducted for up to five years, subject to the ceiling each year.

* * *

2017 2018
Deductible subject to various AGI limits
Increased limitation for cash contributions
    from 50% to 60%
All other AGI limits unchanged

It's important to remember that changes that are highlighted in the TCJA that affect individuals may also affect business tax as well.

- There is a new income deduction in the TCJA that affects sole-proprietors, self-employed individuals, partners in partnerships, and shareholders in S Corporations. In this deduction, if eligible, persons can be granted a deduction of up to 20% of their reported business income. The income guidelines for eligibility are below $315,000 for joint income tax returns, and below $157,000 for the rest of taxpayers returns.

- Corporate tax rates were lowered by the TCJA to a flat 21% of taxable income.

- Businesses are allowed to have a net operating loss (NOL) if the amount of deductions is higher than its business income for the reporting year. The TCJA limits the net operating loss deduction to

80% of the taxable income for the year rather than the full 100% .

- Bicycle commuting reimbursement was added in the TCJA. Employers can now deduct qualified bicycle commuting reimbursements as a business expense through the year 2025. These reimbursements should be included in the employee's wages.

- S Corporations may want to consider changing over to C Corporations because of the flat C Corporation 21% flat tax rate as previously mentioned.

- Some S corporations may find it beneficial to convert to C corporations because of the new, flat 21 percent C corporation tax rate. The recent changes make two modifications to existing law for a C corporation.

11

COMMON TAX MISTAKES AND FAQS

To help avoid mistakes as a business owner, you should keep up on all things taxes for your business throughout the entire year. Waiting until it's tax season to try and make sense of a whole year's worth of business is a disaster waiting to happen. Keep accurate records and keep them current! We can't state that enough.

With that being said, filing taxes is a complicated process and mistakes can and likely will happen at one time or another.

Some common mistakes that small businesses make when it comes to taxes.

KEEPING EXPENSES SEPARATED

As a small business owner, it's important that you keep your business and personal expenses separated. This is a common error committed by small business owners. Remember to clearly document when something is a business expense.

LATE FILING AND LATE PAYMENTS

Another common mistake is filing returns late. Late filing, even if you have filed for an extension, is a bad thing. Fees and penalties are the last thing you want incurred upon you as a small business owner. There is really no excuse for late filing. Keep your documentation up throughout the year and have things ready by the due date, if not earlier.

Paying your taxes late is another big no-no when it comes to dealing with the IRS as a small business (or as anyone). Again, just like with late filing, fees and interest can pile up quickly. If you have been paying quarterly estimated tax, hopefully you have been keeping up on those payments throughout the year.

UNDERPAYING ON ESTIMATED TAXES

Speaking of payments, it is also a common error for businesses to underpay on their estimated taxes. When you are figuring what your estimated taxes should be for the year, make sure you are taking everything into consideration when estimating your business income and tax calculations so that your estimated tax that you fall on is close to what you will actually end up owing for the year.

UNDERREPORTING OR OVERREPORTING BUSINESS INCOME

If you make the mistake of over or under reporting your business's income, you're basically asking the IRS to audit you. It is also possible that you could be charged with fraud if the case is severe enough.

Mistakes can happen when making calculations. This is again another example of the importance of accurate record keeping.

If you make an honest mistake, you can still file a correction form to get things fixed and accurate on your filings.

FAILING TO DEPOSIT EMPLOYMENT TAXES ON TIME

When you run a business that has employees, you are responsible for withholding employment taxes and depositing them through EFTs (electronic funds transfers) to the government. Failing to deposit your employment taxes on time can result in your business being fined and having to pay a penalty.

Make sure you are keeping a schedule on when to do this and keeping up on the task.

NOT PLANNING AHEAD

When working with a tax professional, you can get advice with them on how to plan ahead during your business's tax year so that you are prepared for everything come tax season. We don't just mean get advice on how to properly keep your books, or how to keep up your payroll and employment tax info, etc. What we mean here is, work with them on identifying deductions you could use to your advantage throughout the year, as well as planning ahead for what is expected for your taxes so you don't end up with a huge unexpected

ARE THEY AN EMPLOYEE OR A CONTRACTOR?

Believe it or not, people often confuse contractors for employees when they are filing business taxes. Let's clear this one up.

Employees are actually hired and work for your business, have filled out W4 forms and you will give them a W2 at the end of the tax year.

Contractors are workers that are contracted to do work for your business but are not actually employed by your business. They do not fill out W4 forms when starting to work with you.

You can't designate a worker, including your own self, as an employee or independent contractor just by the issuing a Form W-2 or Form 1099-MISC. It does not matter whether the person works full time or part time. You should use Form 1099-MISC, Miscellaneous Income PDF (PDF) to report payments to others who are not your actual employees. You should use Form W-2 to report wages, car allowance, and other compensation for employees.

NOT CAPITALIZING ON DEDUCTIONS

It may seem like extra work, but deductions are worth the effort! Would you skip out on someone handing you a thousand dollars? I think not. You could end up deducting that much and potentially even more if you take the time to look into what you can claim for business deductions.

Honestly, the best thing you can do for your business is to hire an accountant or tax professional to help with your tax return. They will know what to look for and what is available when it comes to tax credits and deductions.

NOT APPLYING PROPER LIMITATIONS ON DEDUCTIONS

If you're using a deduction, remember the limitations that it has! If you don't, you're asking for an audit, as well as possibly having to pay back whatever extra you weren't entitled to. An example would be if you are deducting a business meal but forgot that only 50% was deductible. Or if you are claiming startup costs but forgot the limitation was $5,000.

Always know everything there is to know about deductions that you are choosing to take, most importantly, their limits.

FORGETTING TO TAKE ADVANTAGE OF THE QBI

The QBI or Qualified Business Income deduction, is a common thing for small business owners to forget about. While it's not technically a deduction per se, it is a tax break available for owners of pass-through business structure entities and it's based on the business income. The amount of the QBI will vary depending on income, the type of business structure, and the type of business you are in.

FAILING TO KEEP A MILEAGE RECORD

Countless business owners use their personal vehicles for business reasons from time to time. At the same time, countless business owners forget to keep a mileage record in order to deduct miles according to IRS rules. See IRS Publication 463 for more info on this one.

FORGETTING ABOUT RETIREMENT PLANS

Just because you are a small business owner doesn't mean that you shouldn't have a great retirement plan in place for your future. Believe it or not, having contributions to a retirement plan is a great way to lower your current tax liabilities. Work with a professional financial planner to make sure that you are using a retirement plan that is right for you and your small business.

There could also be a tax credit that you could qualify for. The Solo 401(k) plan allows for the largest contributions when you are running a small business.

The other mistake when it comes to retirement plans is to not contribute enough to them. Retirement contributions are usually considered pre-tax, which makes things a little bit easier on the pocketbook. Best practices when it comes to just how much you should save are anywhere between 10% - 20% of your annual income.

FREQUENTLY ASKED QUESTIONS

Q. *If my partnership or corporation had no income for the year, do I still have to file an information return or income tax return?*

A. For domestic partnerships, you do not have to file an information return if you have not received any gross income or paid or incurred any amount that is treated as a credit or deduction for tax purposes.

For foreign partnerships, you do not have to file an information return if you have no gross income connected with your trade or business in the US, have no gross income from sources in the US, and you are not making an election.

Q. *I am a sole proprietor. Do I need to get an employer identification number (EIN)?*

A. Sole proprietors who do not have employees do not need an employer identification number. While you are not required to have one, you can get one if you want to. When it comes to taxes, your social security number acts as the identifying number for the taxes for your business.

Q. If I use my own home for my business, can I deduct the expenses?

A. To deduct expenses related to the part of your home used for business, you must meet specific requirements. Even then, your deduction may be limited.

You must use part of your home:

- Exclusively and regularly as your principal place of business,
- Exclusively and regularly as a place where you meet or deal with patients, clients, or customers in the normal course of your trade or business,
- In the case of a separate structure which isn't attached to your home, exclusively and regularly in connection with your trade or business,
- On a regular basis for storage of inventory or product samples for use in your trade or business of selling products if your home is the only fixed location of the trade or business,
- For rental use, or
- As a daycare facility.

Q. What are the due dates for filing tax returns for a business?

A. Different business entities may have tax return due dates that are not actually April 15th. Not all businesses use the calendar year for their tax year.

- *Sole Proprietorships* - Due date is the 15th day of the fourth month after the end of the tax year in question (typically April 15th)
- *Partnerships* - Due date is typically the 15th day of the third month after the end of the tax year in question
- *C Corporations* - Can use calendar or tax year. Due date is the 15th day of the fourth month after the end of the tax year in question
- *S Corporations* - Usually are required to use the calendar year unless there is a business reason for having it different than that. Due date is typically the 15th day of the third month after the end of the tax year in question

* * *

Q. *Are the partners in my partnership considered employees of our business?*

A. No. When you are a partner in a partnership, you are actually considered to be self-employed when it comes to performing services within your partnership.

Q. *As a sole-proprietor, how do I pay Medicare and Social Security taxes and report my income?*

A. When you are a sole-proprietor, you use Schedule C on Form 1040 or 1040-SR to report your expenses and income info from your sole proprietorship. If your net income from self-employment from all of your businesses is more than $400, you'll need to use Schedule SE on Form 1040 or 1040-SR to figure your tax that you owe. The self-employment (SE) tax includes Social Security and Medicare taxes.

If the IRS audits your company, you're still responsible for proving business expenses claimed on your taxes.

Q. *What happens if my records are lost, stolen, or destroyed?*

A. When records are lost or stolen, your first reaction should be to inform anyone whose sensitive information may be at risk. For example, if payroll records have gone missing, inform your employees that their SSN might have been exposed.

If your records are unrecoverable, you should do your best to reconstruct all records that justify business tax deductions. Contact your vendors and financial institutions, who should have copies of your business documents.

Q. Should I save this [insert obscure document name here]?

A. If you ever doubt whether a business record is worth keeping, save it. Ask a tax professional or attorney when you're unsure if a record is important.

The IRS usually audits less than 1% of individual and corporate returns submitted, so don't live in fear of an IRS audit. But if your business is chosen, they'll require proof for all income, deductions, and credits you report on your taxes.

Without the proper documentation, you may face an increased tax liability and a negligence penalty equal to 20% of your underpayment.

CONCLUSION

We've made it! That was a lot of information. We hope that you will use this book as a reference for your future needs when it comes to all things small business taxation and operations when it comes to bookkeeping, record keeping, etc.

Take advantage of that glossary in Chapter Two to remind yourself what certain terms mean as they come up in real time. Browse the FAQ section of the last chapter to see if that question you have is referenced. If not, it's probably somewhere else within as well.

As a small business owner, you know that taxes aren't simple and that tax code wasn't made for just anyone to be able to interpret it. Hopefully now that you've read through this e-book, you have a good foundation of terms and knowledge to build on.

We went over the tax basics in chapter one and gave you information about taxes in general, why we have them and what they are and how they are applied within our government. Then our list of common terminology with taxation and accounting is something that we hope will come in handy many times over for you as you operate.

A history of the IRS and the ten commandments in very little but complex detail gives you an idea of how the agency works within our government, and how it is supposed to work for us as individuals as well as business owners.

Tax reform and the details of the TCJA while painfully detailed are a necessary addition because the TCJA was the biggest tax reform in recent history and changed so many things.

We hope you learned a lot about record keeping strategies, bookkeeping strategies and reports, software necessities, and how long to keep your records, as well as how to keep documents sorted and organized.

Learning about the five different main types of taxes that have to do with small business is a huge step in helping you understand what you can be taxed, why you are being taxed, and how to deal with being taxed under those categories.

When you have employees or contractors, we went over how to deal with employment taxes, and the differences between actual employees and a person who is contracted to do work for you, as well as the different types of forms to use for each, and your responsibilities when it comes to taxes for each.

And then let's talk deductions and credits. We hope we gave you some hope! There are so many deductions and credit out there for you as a business owner. Going through the common types of deductions you can take, whether it's on your home office, your startup costs, travel and meal expenses, your car, etc, we hope that you take our advice and find that qualified tax professional that you can work with throughout the year and plan ahead for whatever you think might be applicable for your business during your upcoming tax year.

As a small business owner, you know firsthand that when it comes to taxes, there is no such thing as simple. The tax code can be a challenge to navigate for even the most business savvy of us all. It's not uncommon for people to miss out on things such as deductions or credits that could have saved them thousands. Or even worse, end up with errors or late returns that cost you extra in fees and fines, and let's face it, any unexpected cost in a small business can throw things out of whack in a snap.

In this guidebook, we will help you understand all of the basics you need to know about taxes as a small business owner, and give you strategies to lower your taxes in a legal way.

We'll go over Tax Basics first so to start off with, you'll have the groundwork in your mind for the more detailed info, as well as some of the common terminology associated with Taxation and Accounting. Then, we can't talk taxes without the good ol' IRS, so we've dedicated a chapter to the agency to give you a little bit of history and background on what exactly it is that they do there.

The next few chapters will be filled with important information that is specific to your small business taxes, including some great tips and tricks to help you out along the way. Then finally, we'll end with discussing Tax Reform and how taxes can change from year to year with new legislation passing through Congress.

We'll end with giving you some insight into the most commonly encountered mistakes that small business owners make when filing their taxes, as well as a frequently asked questions section for your review.

As a business owner, I know firsthand that learning about the information you are about to read in this book will help you understand your small business as a whole and in a way that you might not have before.

By knowing how to properly navigate taxation on a small business, you will not only have the peace of mind that you are doing things correctly and can have confidence when it comes time to turn in that return, but you will also reap the benefits by gaining a good credit rating as a business. This is huge, and will show that you and your business are committed to the social responsibility of contributing to the success of your country.

With all of this comes an increase in the chance that your business will be strong and successful.

That all sounds great, right? We have faith that after reading our book, you will truly understand how taxes work, how they apply specifically to your type of small business, and how to lower them so that you can earn more revenue.

If you don't know what you're doing when it comes to taxes as a business owner, you run the risk of harming your business.

What are you waiting for? Buy this book now and become the expert in small business tax that can take their business forward with confidence, and a little extra padding in those pocketbooks.

The need for a qualified tax professional was mentioned a lot and there is a reason for that. Getting the professional help that you need to capitalize on everything that is available to you and your business is just a no brainer. It's worth it! Do it! Go find somebody! And make sure you review what you should be looking for in the process.

Hopefully you learned from the section listing common mistakes people make on their taxes. Learn from others! Check and double check your information.

Keep things. Don't throw stuff out. Have the stuff you need for an audit. Know what your rights are when it comes to going through an audit.

We have faith that now that you've read our book, you will truly understand how taxes work, how they apply specifically to your type of small business entity, and how you can lower your tax so that you can earn more revenue. And you know how to keep an eye on your business's health by running frequent profit and loss statements, at least once a month, and will have an active hand in your bookkeeping processes.

If you don't know what you're doing when it comes to taxes as a business owner, you run the risk of harming your business. Now that you've gotten this far, you're actually on the opposite track and have a good start towards growing your business and its financial well-being.

You are on the road to being a small business tax expert! Keep learning and keep up on updates and changes along the way. Take the advice of that tax professional and keep in touch with them throughout the year and not just at tax time. With all the knowledge and tools, you can reference here in this book, you should be well on your way to having a successful and healthy small business. We wish you well!

CPSIA information can be obtained
at www.ICGtesting.com
Printed in the USA
LVHW082302110321
681328LV00006B/151

9 781914 108181